AN

INTRODUCTION TO THE STUDY

OF

HINDUISM

AN
INTRODUCTION TO THE STUDY
OF
HINDUISM.

(A STUDY IN COMPARATIVE RELIGION)

BIPIN CHANDRA PAL

GYAN

Published by

GYAN

Gyan Publishing House
5, Ansari Road
Daryaganj, New Delhi-110002
Phone: 011-47034999, 9811692060
E-mail: books@gyanbooks.com

Distribution Network
gyanbooks.com
India, USA, Canada, UK, Australia, France

ISBN: 978-81-212-8975-7 (PB)
First Published,1908

2nd Impression 2023

Printed at: Gyan Press, Delhi.

AN INTRODUCTION TO THE STUDY OF HINDUISM

AUTHOR: BIPIN CHANDRA PAL

AN INTRODUCTION TO THE STUDY OF HINDUISM.

(A STUDY IN COMPARATIVE RELIGION)

BY

BIPIN CHANDRA PAL

Written during his confinement in Calcutta and Buxar.

Calcutta.

PRINTED BY S. C. GHOSE AT THE LAKSHMI PRINTING WORKS.
64-1 & 64-2 SUKEA'S STREET.

PREFACE.

These pages were written during my confinement in the Presidency and Buxar Central Jails. They are published just as they came out of the Prison gate.

I desire to take advantage of this opportunity to thank Major Mulvany of the Presidency and Captain Macmillan of the Buxar Central Jail, for the interest they took in my literary labours, that enabled me to write these pages in peace and with pleasure.

CALCUTTA,
August 18, 1908.

BIPIN CHANDRA PAL.

CONTENTS.

ओं

——इहा आमि किछुइ ना जानि,
ये तुमि कहाओ सेइ कहि आमि वाणी।
तोमार शिक्षाय पड़ि येन शुकपाठ;
साक्षात् ईश्वर तुमि, के बुझे तोमार नाट?
हृदये प्रेरण कर, जिह्वाय कहाओ वाणी;
कि कहिव भाल मन्द किछुइ ना जानि॥

—चैतन्य महाप्रभु प्रति रामानन्दवाक्यम्।
चै: च: मध्यलीला, ८म प:

OM

Nought, excepting this I know
That what from my lips doth flow
Is what thou bid'st me say.
And what I pour from out my throat,
Parrot-like I learn by rote
From thee Lord! each day.
A present God thou art, and none
Can fathom what by thee is done
In sport or playful mood.
This heart with thoughts thou e'er dost fill
This tongue with speech providest still,
I know not ill or good.

The Study of Hinduism.

CHAPTER I.

What is Hinduism?

§ 1.

Its General Value.

Its complexity

What is Hinduism? The question has not, we are afraid, been satisfactorily answered as yet. Not to speak of foreigners whose knowledge must necessarily be more or less superficial, even our own scholars have not as yet cared to render an exhaustive and clear answer to it. Hinduism includes so many things, means so much, and at the same time, one might say almost so little, that though the name has become pretty familiar all over the world, the thing is still more or less unknown to and un-understood by most people. It is a religion: but there are people who would not even call it a religion at all. They understand by it a social economy and nothing more, and judged from certain stand-points, their views would be hard to controvert. A religion Hinduism is not. One might as well take Islam and Christianity and Judaism and the religion of Zoroaster, and that of Confucius, and Taoism, with a good deal of what is known as religion even among primitive peoples, and forming a compendium of all these, call it a religion. In Hinduism you find elements that coincide with the essentials of most other world-religions, from the lowest to the highest, standing in a mysterious and profound unity. Worship of gods and godesses like those of Smallpox and Cholera, or even of the Plague; incantations to Sylvan deities, offerings to ancestors, all these are found here standing side by side with the mysteries of the Trinity and the Divine Incarnation, both not less mysterious, though perhaps they might appear to some at least, as far more rational than the essential dogmas of Christianity,—the theosophy of the Mystics and the transcendental emotionalism of a Hafez, an Omarkhayam or a Madame Guion. The contradictions of tenets, the complexities of disciplines, the varieties of cultures, that go to form what we know as Hinduism today, are absolutely bewildering, and we cannot blame people for having failed to discover the unity that underlies these.

This very complexity, however, offers to the students of the science or, more strictly speaking, the philosophy of religion, a most interesting subject of study and investigation in this great world-religion. It may justly claim to be somewhat of an epitome of all world-religions, and the history of religious evolution may be traced in it almost from beginning to end, so far as that end has been yet reached by man. And the value of it, to the student of religion, lies in the fact that in almost all its phases, Hinduism is still a living thing. What you discover as fossils of bygone ages in some of the other religions, you may find, perhaps, in this curious system as almost a living specimen, by which you can, therefore, better understand and more carefully and correctly interpret the mystic and mysterious records of other times and other systems—dogmas and disciplines that having fallen into disuse, have lost their key altogether.

An interesting study

The late Professor Max Muller was, therefore, essentially right in his attempt to start his Science of Religion, practically, with an examination of the earlier records of the religion of the Hindus. It was due, no doubt, to his oriental and especially his Vedic studies. Largely it was due also, we believe, to his special theory regarding the origin and growth of the so-called religious sentiment

An adequate Source of Historical Study.

which found such ample support from certain aspects of Vedic and Upanishadic Hinduism. Both these had their limitations, and his conception regarding the evolution of religion needs considerable amendment and correction no doubt, but inspite of it all, he was intuitively on the right track when he sought for the key for the elucidation of the mysteries of human religions, in the experiences of the Hindu people. We do not, however, mean to suggest by this that the other races had not this key themselves, or that the Hindus have, in any supernatural sense, been a chosen people of God as the Hebrews are described in the Christian Scriptures. By no means so. All that we mean is, as already mentioned above, that while the other religions have passed beyond their earlier stages, Hinduism, as known to us, has not done so, though it has reached in some parts, the stages wherin even the most advanced Christian or Mahomedan religious consciousness stands to-day. We mean that Hinduism is not like some of the great historical religions, an individual religion so to say, but it is a community or a family of religions, some in lower and earlier, some in higher and more advanced stages of growth. Indeed, it is this peculiarity that distinguishes ethnic types of religion from the credal types. All credal religions grew out of some ethnic religion : Buddhism grew out of Hinduism, Christianity out of Judaism, and Islam out of the old Arab ritualism and idolatry. And Hinduism, Judaism, as well as the ancient religion of Arabia, are all ethnic religions, that owned their peculiarities to the peculiar race characteristics, both mental and social, of the particular ethnic groups with which they stood related, and that took their special lines of evolution under the influence of their special nature surroundings, of their social contacts and conflicts with and accretions from their neighbouring groups of humanity. These ethnic religions are always exclusive, counterminious with the particular ethnic groups related to them, refusing accession to their ranks, by mere religious conversion, from other ethnic groups. Ethnic religions are, therefore, also extremely tolerant of other ethnic religions. Not so, however, the credal religions. A definite creed makes these somewhat of a non-national religion: men of all climes and all colour, by accepting the creed may enter its fold, and become members of the same Church or religious denomination. This, however, makes all credal religions more or less rigid, exclusive, and intolerant. The uniformity of creed and the necessary uniformity of discipline and worship and ritual, leave no room for vital divergence of thoughts or cultures within a credal system. Wherever and whenever such divergences do appear, as

Ethnic versus credal religion

they are bound to, owing to the variety of human capacity and the diversity of man's experiences and ideas, they are decreed as heresies. Contradictory things cannot, therefore, find place in credal religions. Where the ante-credal stage is remembered and the ancient and preparatory process of evolution still recognised as sacred and divine, as is done by Christianity, it is preserved as the Old Testament,—an old law, and old ideal, which was good in the olden time, but practically superseded by or subsumed into the new, as childhood is superseded by and subsumed into youth, and youth is done by and into maturity. The old exists as a memory, which may be cultivated for the deepening of love or quickening of gratitude ; but for all that it is not the living present, and has not, therefore, a substantiality just now. Though transcending the limitations of ethnic codes and characters, and therefore assuming a kind of universality, yet credal religions for the new exclusiveness they develop, which is far more rigid in one way, because of its claims to absolutism, than the social but otherwise tolerant exclusivism of ethnic system —cannot find us a key to the elucidation of the infinite variety of human rites and human beliefs. Ethnic systems are somewhat better guides in this matter.

When an ethnic system reaches the universal stage, directly without passing through the mediating credal stage, its value as a key to the solution of the mysteries of the religious experiences of man is simply. immeasurable. It stands then as a living museum of human religions, where the diligent student may study the dead with the help of the living, and interpret the past in the light of the present.

(*a*) A key to the religious experiences of men

The study of Hinduism has, however, apart from this general value to the student of religious Philosophy, a special value to our age. The religious thoughts and ideals of humanity are passing through strange and mighty transformations around us. Not to speak of Europe, even in what has hitherto been regarded as the sleepy and changeless land of the Orient, human culture seems to be running fast into new channels, revolutionising ancient ideals and institutions everywhere. New influences are at work creating new problems; new thoughts and new knowledge are spreading, quickening new doubts, and working up new conflicts that demand everywhere a new synthesis and settlement. In Persia we have not only new political forces pushing themselves up for a democratic constitution, but new religious movements as well, one of which, that of Babism at least, has already made itself heard outside the Kingdom of the Shah. In Afganistan, the working

(*b*) Special value of the study in this transition period

of the new leaven is seen in the ideals and activities of the young prince who rules her destinies. Not to speak of Japan, which openly entered into the larger life of modern humanity, upon her own rights. Even China, the eternally changeless, is throbbing under the pressure of new thoughts and aspirations which, though the details are so far as known to us, could not but create fresh doubts and raise fresh demands for a re-interpretation and re-adjustment of the old life and religion of the people. In India the religious thought and life of the people are passing through the throes, it seems, of a new birth. Hinduism and Islam have both felt the shock of the new world-thoughts and world-ideas, and have, somewhere consciously and openly and some where secretly and unconsciously, been adapting themselves to the new forces and conditions about them. The Hindus, bewildered by the sudden influx of alien ideas and ideals, seem as yet to have scarcely had the needful peace and leisure, to take a full and correct measure either of their old ideals or of the new ones ; and while some are trying to embrace the new to the prejudice of the old, and others are seeking to cling with the tenacity of unreasoning faith to the old, to the entire exclusion of the new, the religious life and thought of the nation at large seem to be slowly but surely breaking out of their old moorings, without competent knowledge or guidance. It is an age of universal questioning and universal doubt; and re-statement of the old verities of life has become imperative, to settle these at rest, in every part of the civilized world. A study of Hinduism, in the light of the highest culture of the times, is absolutely necessary for the purpose of this re-statement, to the Hindus themselves.

(c) Its Special Value to the Western students in solving their problems

Such a study has also, we hold, a special value even to the modern western students and thinkers. There are many problems of modern religious thought and life in Europe and America and even problems affecting the very future of modern Western civilisation and humanity upon which Hindu experience and Hindu ideals may possibly throw much helpful light. Hindu theology has, it seems, passed through a good deal of the trials through which Christian theology seems to be passing to-day. The conflicts of science and scripture, of reason and revelation, of ritualism and ethicism, of Popery and Protestantism, not to mention the profounder problems concerning the Personality and the Incarnation of God and the religio-ethical problems of Divine Immanence and Providence and human freedom and responsibility, —problems before which modern Western thought seems so often to sit down almost in utter despair, leading some to abandon reason altogether and seek refuge in unreasoning and unquestioning faith, and others to give themselves up to a so-called rational, but essentially materialistic view of life ;—all these or most of them in some shape or other seem to have been faced and more or less satisfactorily solved by the ancient and mediæval Hindus. All their solutions may not be acceptable to our age. It would, indeed, be too much to expect such absolute and unerring illumination from ancient experience anywhere, for the solution of modern problems. Our age is diflerent from theirs. The forms of our thinking are, also, more or less different. Though the *character* of our present day problems may be the same as that of the problems that faced people a couple of thousand years ago, still their *centents* are not, and could not in any case be expected to be the same. It is not, therefore, contended that the Christian consciousness of our age will be able to solve its complex problems by bodily accepting the solutions of similar problems that may have satisfied the ancient or mediæval Hindus. Yet at the same time we do claim for a careful and reverent study of Hinduism this much, at least, that it is capable of furnishing valuable hints and suggestions, by working up which even modern Western thought might find its way made a bit clearer than before, and might thus, arrive at more satisfactory conclusions, on some points, than what it has hitherto succeeded in doing.

Such a Study has already broadened and deepened Christian thought

In fact, it would be impossible to deny that the study of non-Christian systems, and more particularly of Brahmanical philosophy and Buddhistic religion, has already had an almost perceptible influence in the broadening and possibly even the deepening of modern Christian thought. The strongest note in current of religious life and thought, on both sides of the Atlantic, is undoubtedly that of Divine Immanence. The speculative philosophy of the last century and the highest generalisations of modern science have both contributed very materially, no doubt, to bring about this result. But the influence of Oriental researches seems to have been almost as effective, in helping this somewhat novel thought-movement in Latin Christianity especially in its spiritual aspects,—an influence that has received the spiritual ideals that had been contributed by Greek thought and more particularly by the Alexendrian Fathers, to the growth and expansion of Christian-thought and piety in the earlier centuries. And yet the deeper notes of Hinduism have not as yet been sounded by any of these European Orientalists. The best of them have only presented partial views of this great world-system. The interpreters of Hinduism among our own people also have either been too much under the influence of modern Materialism, miscalled rationalism, or too blind and unreasoning adherents of ancient mysticism. And both these, rank Rationalism and blind bigotry, are equally unfitted for the work which they seem to have laid out before them.

Its influence already recognised by Western Scholars

Indeed, the need of a critical and intelligent study of Hinduism has been recognised by Western scholars from the days of Sir William Jones, Colebrook, Horace Hayman Wilson, J. Moore and others. And Christian scholars and missionaries have now and again applied themselves to this work during the last hundred years, and more. Even the Hindus are beholden to some of them for their own revived interest in the study of their own literatures. They owe a special debt of gratitude to Sir William Jones, Colebrook, Wilson and Muir, for their researches into their ancient books, and the rites and creeds of even their existing sects and denominations, a good deal of which had lain even beyond their own knowledge so long. But these scholars, though great linguists and painstaking and well-read Oriental students, were not philosophers and they could not therefore properly interpret the meaning and significance of what they so faithfully described or translated. Their successors in the study of Hindu-religion have many of them been Christian Evangelists, and these had no doubt, something of a philosophy of religion with them; but it has been only Christian Philosophy, the generalisation of a different kind of religious thought and experience, allied to a somewhat different type of piety, and their sectarian philosophy has necessarily been able to render them but little help in the interpretation of a foreign system. To most of them what did not run on all fours with Christian dogma or Christian ethics,

Though but inadequately

was necessarily an untruth or an evil and what did seem to do so must have been due to Christian influence. At best, in their estimate the Hindu records referred only to "The unknown God.

Max Muller's interpretation limited by the narrow method of his Philosophy of Religion

Professor Max Muller's was, without doubt, an attempt not merely towards a wider propagation of Hindu lore, but also at a rational and modern, that is scientific and philosophical, explanation of it. His is, so far, the only interpretation of Hinduism that has been attempted for the English speaking peoples at any rate. But the late Professor's interpretation of Hinduism suffers from the limitations of his particular Philosophy of religion, and equally also from the somewhat narrow view that he took of both the comparative and the historic methods upon which, as a matter of course, he had sought to build up that philosophy. It seems, indeed that Professor Max Muller's theological studies grew out of his philological studies and he therefore sought naturally, to apply the same kind of comparative examination to theology as had rendered such excellent results in establishing an organic kinship, for instance, between Sanskrit and Greek and Latin, in the domain of philology. He followed his German masters and fellow-workers in recognising in one common pre-historic stock, the origin of the Hindu, the Greek, the Roman, the Tueton, and the Saxon and other European races. The linguistic affinity was too marked and unerring to be ignored. So far he was on the right track. But Professor Max

Based on Linguistic affinity merely

Muller's philology stopped short of the fundamental philosophy which it suggested and which alone could fully explain it What is the significance of this common lingustic structure? This is a question which does not seem to have troubled Professor Max Muller further than to suggest that people who speak languages that reveal an original structural unity or affinity, must have at one time, lived together and belonged to one and the same race or tribe.

And yet, the close and organic affinity that he seems to have recognised between thought and language should have revealed a much profounder significance in the affinity between Sanskrit and Greek and Latin and other languages of the Indo-European group, than what Professor Max Muller seems to have fully realised, or at least than what he cared to utilise in building up his so-called science of comparative religion. The discovery of this structural affinity among these different languages is a thing of supreme value to the student of comparative religion. For the structure of a language reveals the original structure of the thought,—the primordial cast of mind—of those who have been using that language from pre-historic times. Linguistic affinity implied affinity of a deeper kind,—namely, thought affinity. It meant that people to whom this family of languages belonged have, from pre-historic times, been approaching the same world-problems, practically from the same mental stand-point. And the wonderful affinity that the study of the primitive religions of these peoples discovered in the fundamental religious conceptions, could thus, be very easily explained by this thought-affinity. And had the learned Professor approached the fundamental problems of his so-called Science of Religion from this view-point, his contribution to the study of Comparative Religion would have been far more valuable and puəuring, and his interpretation of Hinduism also would have been richer by far and more

But Max Muller could not realise that linguistic affinity pre-supposes thought affinity

satisfactory than what they are generally found to be.

---

§ 2.

Max Muller's Presentation of Hinduism.

The Origin of religious consciousness in man ascribed to the innate sense of the Infinite first quickened by his nature surroundings

The fundamental problem before Comparative Religion is the origin of the religious consciousness in man. Professor Max Muller sought to solve it by ascribing it to an innate sense of the Infinite in man; and this intuition of the Infinite in man was first quickened by his nature-surroundings. This is the fundamental idea of Professor Max Muller'sphilosophy of religion. Possessed with this one idea, he sought for its illustrations in the earliest religious experiences of man as recorded in Sanskrit and Greek literature, and starting from this Nature-Religion he sought to trace the evolution of the religious sentiment, up to what he called Theosophy,—culminating in the consciousness of God as the Soul of the Universe and the Self of man, throwing, in the course of this up-building of his Science of Religion, considerable light, now and again, upon the affinities between, not only Vedic and Hellenic religions,—but even between the more advanced forms of Hinduism, Christianity and Islam. But valuable as his history of Hinduism undoubtedly is, it is, after all, more or less partial, and does not cover the whole field, nor advance the solution of the most perplexing problems of this strange and weird system.

His charming picture of the Particularism or Naturalism of the Hindus

Professor Max Muller, more perhaps than any other European Oriental scholar, has himself, however, raised some of these very perplexing problems before the modern student of human, and specially, of Hindu religion. In his studies of the Vedic religion, he has presented the world with a charming picture of the particularistic or naturalistic religion of the primitive Hindus. And one can understand this phase of religious evolution more or less. This sort of Naturalism or Particularism is not peculiar to ancient Hinduism alone. For religion in the earlier stages is always and everywhere of a Particularistic or Naturalistic type. We find these Nature-deities in ancient Greece and Rome. They are common to all Aryan religions. And we find traces though not of a Naturalistic stage, but distinctly of a Particularistic one, even in Semitic records. Even the so-called Monotheism of the ancient Hebrews is pretty generally admitted, by modern scholars, to have been really not *monotheism*, which would preclude the very possibility of more than one God, but simply *Monolatry*, (1) which, without denying the existence

(1) See Shultz---"Old Testament Theology" Vol. I.

of other gods, simply adhered absolutely to the worship of one God. Indeed, the existence of these other gods,—"Strange Gods," as they are called,—is never denied absolutely in the old Hebrew records. In the Psalms we have it that—

"In the council of the gods sat God, where the existence of the other gods is not denied, but only the supremacy of God—the Lord Almighty of Israel, over them is declared and asserted. In the earlier records we find Taleveh, in fact, struggling to secure and prove his superiority to these other gods. He is there only one God among many gods. Other peoples have their own gods, and so long as these peoples do not come into conflict with the people of Israel, the God of Israel does not come into conflict with their gods. The God of Israel does not, in the earlier records, claim authority over other nations.

A curious characteristic of all Ethnic religions

This, indeed, as we have already pointed out, is the common characteristic of all Ethnic religions. They are all, in the lowest stages, of a particularistic type. And though Vedic or Hellenic particularism differs very meterially from early Hebrew particularism, still the former is not absolutely un-understandable by those whose religious traditions have been more decidedly Semitic than Aryan.

His successful transition from the Vedas to the Upanishads and their Brahma-Jnanam

Thus European students can generally enter into the spirit of Vedic-naturalism and they more or less enjoy the poetry of the religious imagination of the primitive Hindu. When Professor Max Muller worked up his studies from the Vedas to the Upanishads, and presented to the English-speaking peoples, the profoundly spiritual and ethical ideals and cultures of philosophic Hinduism,—what he termed, Theosophy,—and especially as in doing so he tried to explain and interpret the Brahma-Jnanam or Gnosticism of the Hindus, in the terms of Christian gnosticism, seeking to establish some sort of a parallelism between the teachings of the Hindu saints and sages, and those of the Alexandrian Fathers, Oregen, Clement, Tertullion and others, he was able to present something both intelligible and interesting to the European reader. And all this has helped to awaken curiosity, if not to create an interest in Hinduism among a large and increasing class of people on both sides of the Atlantic. We are thankful for all this pioneering work. Indian culture and civilisation owe a debt to Professor Max Muller for all this, which is immense, and must remain always unpaid and unpayable. And it casts no reflection upon the worth of his works to say that some of the most complex problems that these works have raised, have not been satisfactorily

But he has not been able to solve all the problems that he has related

solved by them. Every student and scholar, however valuable their works, and whatever finality might be claimed for some of the results of their labours, must raise questions which either elude their grasp, or which they find it impossible to tackle within the short span of life granted them here below. Professor Max Muller has done more than what has been even attempted by any other person so far, to popularise Hindu thoughts and ideals among English-speaking peoples; and if still a good deal remains yet to be done, it does not reflect upon the richness of his intellect or the breadth of his acquisition, but proves only the depth, the complexity and the vastness of the field in which he laboured with such zeal and such success throughout a life-time.

His work fails to reconcile the early spirituality of the Hindus with the current ceremonials and so called idolatry

Professor Max Muller's presentation of Hinduism seems, owing to this reason, to have as much interested as it has perplexed the English and American reader. For, people have failed, so far, to reconcile the spiritual teachings of Hinduism, which the learned Professor tried to emphasise, with the current ceremonialism and so-called Idolatry of the Hindu people. The problem of this so-called Idolatry is an unsolved problem even to the vast majority of educated Hindus themselves. As for European and

American readers of Professor Max Muller, many of them have even been tempted to regard his interpretations of Hinduism as far-fetched and ingenuous,—the result of a reading of his own advanced views and ideals into the crude utterances of the ancient rhapsodists and mystics of India. And this suspicion has received support from the fact that neither Professor Max Muller, nor, so far as we know, any other European Orientalist has tried to present a consistent and philosophic study of present-day Hinduism, though many have written and spoken very highly of its ancient records, while Christian propagandists have almost uniformly painted the former in the darkest colour possible. And all this conflict and confusion of estimates and interpretations have left Hinduism an unsolved and insoluble riddle to the general European mind.

CHAPTER II.

General Observations.

§ 1 Methods of Study.

A right method of study alone can remove the confusion referred to

What is needed to remove this confusion is a right method of study. In the first place, it must be always borne in mind that Hinduism does not fully explain itself. Nothing, indeed, in the universe ever does so. For, everything is in an almost endless chain of relations and must, therefore, to be fully understood, be interpreted by and through these varied relations. Isolation is not only death, but it is chaos and unreason, in God's world. The particular never can interpret itself; it must, to be rightly understood, be brought under the light of the general or universal. Hinduism is a particularity, it presents a particular class or classes or group or groups of religious phenomena, or spiritual experiences, the real meaning and purpose of which can never be got at, unless they are brought under some general truths or principles. In other words, the study of any particular religion must be entered upon by the light of some general Philosophy of Religion,—which shall sum up the highest generalisations of the religious experiences of mankind.

And the method of study here must, at once, be scientific and philosophical,—scientific, that is, based upon an examination of actual facts and experiences, and its results must be capable, to some extent at least, of verification, and philosophical, that is, have for its back-ground the ultimate generalisation of *all* human knowledge and experience. This combination of science and philosophy is necessary in a right method of investigation of the religious phenomena, for the very simple reason that religion itself is both a science and a philosophy. It is a philosophy because dealing with ultimate principles and verities. It is a science because it aims by various methods and disciplines,—physical and psycho-physical as well as intellectual and moral,—to actualise in life and conduct, the ultimate realities of philosophy. Indeed, religion and philosophy are one. In India, at least, this truth has never been lost sight of. For religion in its theoretic aspect is philosophy: philosophy in the practical side is religion. The methods of investigating the phenomena of religion cannot, therefore, be purely speculative or *a priori*, nor yet absolutely positive or *a posteriori*, but there must be a combination here of both science and metaphysics. Indeed, almost every attempt to build up a Philosophy of Religion, from the time of Hume up to our own days, has partaken, more

The method must be scientific and philosophical

or less, of this dual character; and Prof. Max Muller has even called his Philosophy of Religion, openly and defiantly a Science, and the methods that he adopted in his investigations, though they need considerable correction and amendment,—largely justified the name.

The analysis and classification of experience is the universal end of all science. The science of Religion means a systematised knowledge of religious experience. Its end is or ought to be the analysis and classification of the particular class of human experience called religious; and the science of Religion in seeking this end must follow the approved methods by which it is sought in other departments of human experience. But every science takes for granted the ultimate verities which form the fundamental ground of the particular group of human experience it seeks to investigate. The necessary postulates of Physical science, for instance, are the truth and reality of universal sense-perceptions, that testify to the so-called properties of material objects and prove their existence. It is not the province of this science to examine, analyse, and verify the truth of these perceptions, or discover their real character. The existence of the material world and our relations with that world through our senses, the

A science of religion means a systematised knowledge of religious experiences the ultimate explanation of which rests with metaphysics and philosophy

general trustworthiness of universal sense-testimony, these are the assumptions of Physical Science. It starts with these necessary assumptions. The psychological group of the sciences also do, and must, similarly start with and work upon certain truths, which they must accept on trust, and take for granted. It is the function of philosophy, or strictly speaking, of metaphysics, to investigate, discover and establish the fundamental verities involved in our psychological experiences. And as we ascend in the investigation of our experience from the material to the mental plane,—using this word in its widest sense, to include every department of our inner life, from the mere psychological to the highest spiritual aspects of it,—its dependence upon philosophy or metaphysics increases in a direct ratio. The physical sciences may not trouble themselves with ultimate verities; but yet even those cannot move one step without the aid of Mathematics, and Mathematics, though regarded popularly as the most positive of all the sciences, can not divorce itself altogether from philosophy or metaphysics. Time and Space are the two things with which Mathematics deals, and Time and Space are really unintelligible except in the light of the most profound and abstruse metaphysics. Space is extension, time is succession, and both inhere, so to say, as primary properties, not in the matter but in the mind. Mathematics takes for granted the infinity of both time and space, which is made posisible really by positing an Infinite Mind behind them ; and thus even Mathematics runs dangerously into the bewildering labyrinths of metaphysical speculations. There is, however, a view of the physical sciences, which does avoid philosophy or metaphysics, and for all so-called practical, that is empirical purposes, it may well do so. But the biological group of the sciences cannot as easily do it. For though biology in the lowest stages may possibly avoid psychological investigations, in the higher forms, not mere birth, growth, and decay, with the functions of reproduction, represent the only, and least of all, the highest manifestation of life. In the higher forms, sense-activity is very closely associated with life, and sense-activity cannot be interpreted by biology alone ; but we must seek for its real meaning and significance at the hands of psychology, which is again very intimately related to metaphysics and cannot, indeed, move one single step without it.

And the group of human experiences commonly known as religious cannot by any means, be put on the same level with those that furnish materials for astronomy or physics, or chemistry, or anatomy and physiology, though all these have always had a great influence in shaping man's religious ideals and conceptions. They belong, taking the lowest and least speculative view of them, to the domain of psychology. They are mental or emotional experiences, and are therefore, more directly and intimately allied to philosophy and metaphysics than any others. Philosophy and metaphysics cannot, consequently, be at all ignored in the investigation of these experiences, and any attempt to reduce them to systematised knowledge, must first of all discover their philosophical or metaphysical foundations. The Science of Religion, in other words, must be, as we have already said, different from the other sciences in as much as its treatment must be partly philosophical or metaphysical and partly scientific.

Religious phenomena as psychological are more intimately related to metaphysics and philosophy

Science of religion must presuppose metaphysical and philosophical foundations

---

§ 2. Method of Science of Religion.

In fact, until very recently, theologians and philosophers had almost exclusively followed the *a priori* method in the investigation of religious truths; and any strictly scientific treatment of the subject was all but absolutely inconceivable to our forefathers. David Hume was, perhaps, the first English thinker, who sought to approach the

Hume first applied the *a posteriori* method to the study of religious phenomena

phenomena of human religion from a purely natural, as opposed to a supernatural stand-point. Since then deists and sceptics have occasionally tried, no doubt, to follow in his wake and to trace the origin of the religious consciousness in man to his ordinary physical or psychical experiences, but the standard works on the subject followed still the old *a priori* methods, and the general literature on religion continued, for a long time, to belong to the domain of speculative philosophy. It was only in the last century that "the discovery of Sanskrit," and of the Comparative Method that directly resulted from it, on the one hand, and the birth of the science of anthropology which sought to investigate and classify the primitive life and experiences of humanity and the critical study of the religious records of the different nations of the world, on the other, commenced for the first time to almost revolutionise the old and familiar methods of investigating religious truths. And yet, a little over thirty years ago, even Professor Max Muller had to plead piteously before an enlightened Oxford audience, in justification of what he called his Science of Comparative Religion.

Discovery of the comparative method and birth of anthropology in the last century

Every Science has its own proper methods of investigation. What are the special methods of investigation for the Science of Religion, then? The answer to this question has already been partially anticipated by the assertion of the close and organic relation that this science has to Philosophy or Metaphysics. Observation, experiment, verification, these are the common methods of all science, and these must also, more or less, be applicable to the study of the religious phenomena; we say more or less because the methods of experiment here must be psychological and owing to the almost infinite variety, complexity and subtlety of all mental phenomena the verification of results here must, necessarily, be less positive, and must be examined more in the mass than in isolated or individual cases as is necessary in the case of mere physical or even biological phenomena. But still, any strictly scientific investigation of the religious phenomena cannot altogether ignore these common methods of science. The methods that must, however, be peculiar to the Science of Religion, are the Comparative and the Historic methods, the two worked together, and always under the guidance of the Law of Evolution.

Its method, then, is Histrio-comparative guided by the law of Evolution

Evolution of Religion, however, must follow the universal lines of mental or emotional evolution,—must follow, in other words, the Dialectics of Reason. This necessity is imposed upon Religion by its very nature as both a mental and an emotional

Dialectic Evolution of religion found universally true

phenomenon. As both thought and sentiment move from unity to duality and fulfil themselves in totality, as the movement of Reason is from thesis to antethesis and from antethesis to synthesis in which it finally fulfils and realises itself, as all evolution, in the words of Herbert Spencer, is from homogeniety to differentiation and from differentiation to integration, so also the course of religious evolution whether in the individual or in the race, must be *from* unity or homogeneity or thesis, *through* duality or differentiation or antethesis, *to* totality or integration or synthesis. And this course of evolution which speculative philosophy lays down as the only natural course for the growth of human religions, is found upon a careful stndy of the different world-religions to be what has been actually and universally followed by them. It has been the one universal course of evolution of religion whether in India or Judea, China or Greece.

The Dialectic of reason is a postulate given to these Sciences by Philosophy and it has been fully verified by critical research

This Dialetic is the contribution of philosophy to the Science of Religion. This is, so to say, its primary assumption and like every postulate of science this dialectic is fully verified and justified by a critical study of and research into the actualities of religious history. Whatever methods, whether comparative or historic, we may adopt in the investigation of the phenomena of human religion, their results must always be tested, connected and verified by this Dialectic of Reason, this Law of Evolution. For, the application of this law of mental evolution can alone verify the truth of our interpretations or correct the errors of our assumptions and inferences. This is of special value in the working out of the Comparative Method, in religious investigations. To cite a concrete instance, let us take the so-called idolatry of primitive culture, and the worship of stocks and stones by an advanced people like the Hindus, or the Greeks. A Negro walks out of his hut and stumbles upon a piece of rock or flint, and says—"ta ta"—"thou art here, I did not know," and putting it in his bag, proceeds, on his day's errand. Should he succeed in his errand, he attributes the success to the kindly influence of the rock or flint, brings it back home, and sets it up among the other objects of his reverence or worship, and henceforth it becomes a fetish to him.* Here is distinctly some kind of idolatry. And there is also the so-called stone-god (the sacred black-stone) worshipped by some Hindus. The one form of worship looks, from the outside, very much like the other; and judging from the outside, comparing the two phenomena with one another, one may easily be led

*See Taylor's "Primitive Culture and Early History of Mankind".

to set Negro fetishism and Hindu idolatry on the same plane. The application of the mere Comparative Method would be bound to lead to such a conclusion. But the question is, are all comparisons valid? Does not the validity of comparison, as a method of the investigation of truth, depend upon some fundamental unity existing between the objects or phenomena thus brought up for comparison with one another? The same class of objects or phenomena alone allow valid and scientific comparison between them, and not those that have no such community. Can we put Negro fetishism and Hindu idolatry in the same class? This is the primary question here. And the Historic Method can alone render a correct answer to this question. Negro fetishism and Hindu idolatry can both, no doubt, be classed as religious phenomena; there is thus one common basis between these, to justify comparison. But is this sufficient? The history of Negro fetishism and of Hindu idolatry can alone answer this question. Is there any similarity in their history, in the story of their growth? So the historic method must be brought in to verify or correct the comparative. Nor will this be sufficient. The history of these institutions must be read in the light of evolution; and then,

In such a study as this mere application of the comparative Method to phenomena of different stages without the Historical Method marking the stages of growth and the law of Evolution showing the dialectic movement would be futile and mischievous.

and only then, could we arrive at the truth about them. There is worship of stones among the Negroes, and it is also found among the Hindus. But does a fetishistic interpretation of Hindu idolatry, fit in with the other aspects of the Hindu religion? Religion is only one, though undoubtedly the greatest, of the many concerns of life. It represents only one side of human culture. Do the other sides of Hindu religion, and the other departments of Hindu culture, agree with the religion and the culture of the Negro? If not, how is it that their religion should, even in some part, show such strange similarity? Mere comparison cannot solve the riddle. Isolated similarities or even apparent identities do not justify scientific comparison, and the application of the comparative method to such cases must necessarily produce wrong results.

Take, for instance, again the institution of divorce. Divorce is very common among the primitive races of the Pacific. In India the custom obtains among the hill tribes. Divorce also exists in England and America. Comparing, then, the institution of divorce as existing among the barbarians of the Pacific or the aborigines of India, with that found among Englishmen and Americans, shall we ascribe the same significance to both, and conclude that at least so far as their marriage customs or laws are concerned, the Indian aborigines stand on the same level of higher civilisation and culture as the European races, and are, necessarily, superior so far to the Hindus among whom divorce is unknown? Yet the comparative method alone gives no other result; and it only shows up its utter insufficiency and fallibility unless corrected by the Historic Methods and verified by the general Law of Evolution. In the example under notice, for instance, the application of the Historic Method at once brings out the fact that divorce, among primitive races, is associated with loose marriage bonds, while, among civilised peoples, like those of Europe or America, it exists along with very strict and rigid marriage ties and we at once discover the truth that the meaning of divorce among people whose marriage customs are very loose, and who have not as yet risen, indeed, to a sense of the sanctity of the marital bond, must necessarily be very different from what it signifies among people whose marriage customs have passed through many advanced stages of evolution, and the institution of marriage among whom has reached the state of absolute monogamy. Divorce is common in loose marriage cnstoms, where men and women can unite and be separated almost at their will without any serious let or hindrance from the social authority over them. It is, again, a device, consciously organised to meet an almost dire necessity arising out of the very rigidity of the marital bond and the sancitity of the nuptial relation on strictly monogamous countries. And its meaning, its moral and spiritual significance, differ very widely in the two cases. But this difference is discovered only by those who have studied the history of the institution of marriage and are thoroughly acquainted with the course of its evolution. And it shows that the Comparative Method is a very misleading guide to truth unless associated with the Historic Method, and illumined by the General Law of Evolution of the objects, ideas or institutions to which it is sought to be applied.

There can, therefore, be no valid comparison between Negro-fetishism and the so-called idolatry of the Hindus, because the two do not stand on the same plane of religious history or religious evolution. The one belongs to primitive culture, and fits in well with the general level of intelligence and civilisation of the inhabitants of Tropical Africa. It is not, so far as we know, associated with any refined religious philosophy, nor has it any long course of religious evolution behind it. The other is found in a far higher state of intelligence and culture. It is supported by an abstruse philosophy, however casuistic it may seem to us. It has a course of most wonderful religious evolution behind it. There are indications of a kind of primitive fetishism in the Vedas. But the ceremonialism of current Hinduism stands on an altogether different plane. It is not even what Taylor would call a *survival* of Vedic religion. Hindu idolatry, as we find it to-day, is decidedly post-Vedic. It is positively post-Vedantic as well, developed after the inculcation of the profound gnosticism or *Brahma-jnanam* of the Upanishads. It is an offshoot of Pauranic Hinduism. And the moment we thus trace its history, we find that whatever may be its origin or significance, whatever value may be attached to it as a method of religious or spiritual culture, whatever may have been its moral effect upon the Hindu people, we can by no means class it together with the fetishism of primitive culture. Primitive fetishism, in any case, is not much of a mystery,—Hindu idolatry undoubtedly is. And the mere comparative method will not solve it. It is likely to increase the existing confusion more than ever. What is needed in the study of Hinduism, therefore, as in the study of any other world-religion, is to combine the Comparative with the Historic Method, and work the two together under the guidance of the Law of Religious Evolution.

CHAPTER III.

The Theory of Religious Evolution Logical and Chronological.

§ 1. The Logical Moments.

The evolution of religion means the evolution of man's ideas, sentiments, and activities in relation to God, or whatever may stand to Him, for the time being for that complex concept. It is, therefore, an essentially mental or psychological evolution, and it must consequently follow the dialectic Reason. The progress of this evolution must, in other words, be as we have already stated, from Thesis to Antethesis and from Antethesis to Synthesis, or to use Herbert Spencer's phraseology, from Homogeneity to Differentiation and from Differentiation to Integration. This much must be conceded; but some people have, however, mixed up the logical process with the idea of a chronological succession, and have laid three distinct stages of religious evolution. Even no less a person than Prof. Caird, the present Master of Balliol, has lent himself, unwittingly, to this misconception, by dividing the course of religious evolution into three distinct stages,

The logical process of Evolution is sometimes confused with the Chronological, as appears in Prof. Caird's reference to the three distinct Stages, subjective, objective and the absolute when he really means a logical or dialectic process.

namely, the Objective, the Subjective, and the Universal. * Our first objection here is to the word 'stage' itself, as an exceedingly misleading term to apply to the *process* of evolution, though for want of a more accurate word, it is often, and loosely, used in the literature of evolution. A stage is associated, in the first place, with the idea of a halt, a temporary cessation of movement, and even where there is no halt, it indicates, at any rate, a definite end to what has gone before. But does evolution know anywhere such a halt or rest or separation? In biological evolution are not what are called the lower stages reproduced always, in quicker succession or under subtler forms, in the higher organism? Does not every human organism re-act the whole past of its race, in its growth from the cell to the human fœtus and from the fœtus to the grown up baby, and from the baby to the full-developed man or woman? And is it not the universality of evolution everywhere? If it be said that the word stage means here mere land-marks and is not meant to suggest any acutual halt or separation, even then the idea seems to be incompatible with our conception and knowledge of the law of evolution. A land mark is what marks the progress of a moving thing. It must, therefore, necessarily

* Caird's "Evolution of Religion."

stand outside that thing. But what are called stages of religious evolution do not surely stand outside the evolving religion, but form parts of itself. But in evolution, religion is perpetually changing and cannot have such land-marks or stages in itself, though these may exist outside as memories and records. And if we take up these records again, we find as we shall see, not three but almost countless stages or land-marks of progress in every one of the great world-religions.

The fact, indeed, seems to be that in tracing the evolution of religion, Professor Caird has naturally followed the dialectic of Reason; and his Objective, Subjective, and Universal, are only synonyms for Thesis, Antethesis, and Synthesis or Homogeneity, Differentiation and Integration. As an indication, therefore, of the logical process of the evolution of the religious conciousness this enumeration may well be accepted as unexceptionable. But still, it cannot be denied that it lends itself easily to what may be regarded as a chronological succession, and is, consequently, somewhat misleading.

Indeed, this misconception is likely to arise from the survival among half-educated people of the old pre-Darwinian notion of evolution, as a rectilinear process, which easily admitted of stages that had been reached and left behind. But the modern conception of the evolutionary process is that its movement is not rectilinear but spiral, that it is a progression through what may be called a dual process of evolution and involution that it is marked as moving constantly forward and backward, both these movements in this zig-zag fashion, perpetually leading to a higher point. And this mechanical, and therefore necessarily, very inadequate and imperfect symbol of what is essentially an ideal mental principle, makes the nearest approach to the truth about evolution, on account of its suggesting, if it may not reproduce, the dialectic of Reason. For in the evolution of thought or in the process of reason, Thesis, Antethesis, and Synthesis are not three permanent stages, so that when Thesis is passed and Antethesis is reached, the former is passed for ever, never to recur again, and when through this Antethesis, the third or last stage, that of Synthesis is reached, thought attains its finality and perfection, and further movement of reason comes to an end. By no means so. Thought never attains such absolute perfection. The movement of Reason never reaches finality. Its process has been described of old, as that of eternal generation. And movement is of the very essence of thought—the movement of Reason from Thesis through Antethesis to Synthesis or from Homo-

But the modern conception of Evolution as spiral in its character is likely to bar out such a misconception.

geneity through Differentiation to Integration,—* is the very soul of it. When this movement is stopped, thought or Reason ceases to be. It is the state of what the Buddhists would perhaps call *Nirvana.* It is the state of Undifferentiated Being, what Hegelians call Pure Being, and Pure Being, according to Hegel's dictum, is Pure Nothing. It may be an unconcious, or what some call a super-conscious condition. But religion is a concern, very largely, if not absolutely, of our concious life, and in religious evolution, there can be no such finality as the enumeration of a definite number of its stages of evolution of growth would seem to suggest. Reason or thought moves perpetually and recurrently from Thesis to Antethesis and from Antethesis to Synthesis. There is no point in the history of Thought, wherein this process is absent. And there is no point in the evolution of any religion which is essentially an evolution of Thought or Reason where also this process or Reason is or can be absent. To say that any religion was Objective at the beginning, became Subjective subsequently in the middle, and finally reached

The dialectic movement of thought is eternal and when it ceases, thought ceases with it as in *Nirvana*

The Evolution of a Religion is therefore also not to cease if it is to exist as a living Religion

* "In every act of knowledge" (or thought or reason) "the Self separates itself from itself to return to itself to be itself." Hegel : and this presents the eternal process of Reason.

the Universal stage in the end, is to declare that it has fully and absolutely realised itself, that there is nothing further for it to strive after and attain, and that the Religious Idea has reached its finality, its consummation, its Nirvana here. It means that it has ceased to evolve any more. And to say so is, really, to condemn it beyond the pale of all organic movement and growth, declare it, in other words, to be no more a moving, living religion, but a dead one.

We do not forget that almost all the so-called historical religions—Buddhism, Christianity, and Islam, owing to their credal character, have claimed some sort of a finality for their revelations. But even here, as history shows, there has been growth, if not of the religious ideal, in any case of the religious consciousness of their votaries, through the centuries that they have held sway over the life and thought of a large portion of humanity. The History of all these religions has a story of almost incessant struggles and conflicts to either understand their message or to actualise their ideals and doctrines in life and experience. Even if the fundamental dogmas of Christianity be held to have remained the same since the days of St. Paul or the Councils of Trent or Nice, yet not even the most rigid Christian orthodoxy would for a

Even the credal religions claiming finality for their revelations admit the growth of religious consciousness thereby admitting dialectic Evolution.

moment refuse to admit that there has been all through these centuries a growth in this world of what may be called the Christian consciousness. No one, indeed, can read the history of the Christian Church without noticing the evolution of Christian thought and life through the last two thousand years. The same process of evolution is also seen in the history of both Buddhism and Islam. Even in our day there are what may be called progressive movements in all these credal systems. There is the New Orthodoxy in Anglican Christianity, there is neo-Buddhism in Siam and Ceylon, and there is Babism, the latest phase of change in Islam, in Persia. Indeed, such changes are inevitable. When men's conceptions regarding Nature and society are passing through transformations on all sides, it would be idle to expect that religion alone would remain unaffected by this influx of new world ideas and ideals.

Thus the dialectic process is Eternal and Universal ever repeating itself through the necessary moments

In fact, the history of every religion bears testimony to the perpetual recurrence of the three moments of the dialectic of Reason in them. Commencing with the earliest or Perceptive and Naturalistic state, man's religion proceeds perpetually onward describing what may be called an endless series of elliptical figures in almost incessant succession. Thus what in the present state of our knowledge we have accepted as the earliest state of religious evolution, may be regarded as the state of Thesis or Homogeneity,—though even this may have been, for aught we know, preceded by still more primitive states of evolution; and what we accept now, somewhat arbitrarily, it will have to be admitted,—as the state of Thesis in the religious evolution of the primitive man, may have possibly been itself the Synthesis of a previous circle or series. For we know from subsequent history that the Synthesis of a lower and preceding state, becomes always the Thesis of the next higher and succeeding process. And so on the course of evolution proceeds recurrently and perpetually, from Thesis through Antethesis to Synthesis. And this is so, because of the progressive nature of human thought and human culture.

§ 2 The Stage of Conflicts and Progress.

Religious progress through perpetually recurrent conflict between ancient tradition and mordern experience

The history of religious progress ever so far as we can trace it, is really the story of the recurrent conflicts between ancient tradition and modern experience. Tradition hands down certain dogmas, disciplines, certain ideals, cultures, as true, and binding upon every man to every generation, with the latest interpretations and commendation of these, and they are, at first accepted on trust, and without question. This is the state of thesis. But the new generation also gathers new experiences, either through closer views of its own environments or through foreign contact and influence. And there arises slowly a conflict between new experiences and old traditions, between new truths, and old authorities. This is the state of antethesis. This conflict, however, cannot last for ever. Thought abhors these conflicts and contradictions, and puts forth all its efforts to set these at rest. Victory, however, is never found to belong, in these conflicts, absolutely either to the new or the old. There is always a compromise. A fair settlement is needed by the very character of the combatants. Because the old as well as the new, whatever exaggerations or untruths might be found in the *inferences* mixed up with them, are both results of *actual* experience, and both possess, therefore, the soul of truth. The error or what is condemned as such is in the later interpretations of the old by people who had not the original experience themselves, or in the exaggerated claims and unwarranted inferences of the new. By duly correcting the fanciful and second-hand interpretations on the one side and the exaggerated pretensions or unwarranted inferences on the other, a fair settlement is not difficult to arrive at. There are other ways by which these conflicts are overcome and fresh synthesis arrived at. We find proofs of these in the canons of scriptural interpretation and in the exegetical literature of the different world-religions. But by whatever methods it is overcome, antethesis is never allowed to exist for long anywhere. For thought or reason cannot exist for any length of time in contradiction to itself. Thought-life cannot bear contradictions, its very soul is harmony. The state of antethesis is always a state of unstable equilibrium. It cannot rest on itself, and is, therefore, necessarily followed by some sort of a synthesis that sets all doubts and conflicts at rest for a while, until fresh questionings arise creating fresh conflicts, demanding a fresh settlement or synthesis. This is the general outline of the history of religious evolution. Faith, doubt, settlement or solution of the difficutly, creating a new faith, and again new doubts, new solutions and so on recurrently—this is the universal story of religious progress and evolution, as much in the individual as in the race.

And in the face of this universal story how can we set down the different *stages* of the evolution of religion, as we may, for instance, that of the butterfly. The caterpillar, the chrysalis, the butterfly : these are the stages in the evolution of the latter creature. Can we similarly lay down three definite stages of the evolution of man's religion? Every generation has its own preculiar faiths,—the result of its peculiar experiences, mental, moral, and spiritual,—its own peculiar doubts which it seeks to solve in its own peculiar way leaving an exceedingly complicated legacy of faiths, doubts, and possible solutions for the next. Even if we skip over the minor changes that are being constantly worked in man's conceptions regarding religious duties by his advancing knowledge of Nature and his changing views of himself, even the larger and broader transformations that are preceptible after comparatively long periods of time, scarcely give us materials for such generalisations as will justify our laying down a definite number of stages of universal religious evolution. For the very simple reason that the character of these transformations is not the same, or even is not similar, in all religions.

Resulting in transformations different under different circumstances

In tracing the evolution of Hinduism, for instance, it has been the usual practice with modern students, to take the Vedas, the Upanisads, and the Puranas, as marking its three principal stages of growth. But when we examine the Vedas closely, we find that these cover not one but many stages. Indeed, they indicate a long course of the evolution of Hindu thought and theology. The Vedas are a compilation of *mantras* or what are called Sanhita texts and Brahmans or directions for rituals, interspersed with exegetical interpretations and numerous stories, legends and

Illustrated in the evolution of Hinduism through the Vedas, Upanisads and Puranas each of which involves numerous Stages and Conflicts ancient anecdotes. But even the Sanhita texts of the Vedas, which are regarded as the most ancient portion of these Scriptures, do not refer, it is clear, to any one particular period of the primeval history of the Indo-Aryan family, nor to any definite stage of their mental or social evolution. There are verses in the Rig-Veda, for intance, that very distinctly refers to the time when the Vedic Aryans were engaged in jungle-clearing, that is, when they were in the earliest stage of evolution that sociology or Anthropology has been able as yet to trace in the history of the human race. The view of the jungle-fire as a friend of man, in as much as it "shaves the surface of the earth and clears it of all having growths," like a clever barber, clearly conveys the memory of the times when man was engaged in the arduous work of clearing the earth for his habitation. Side by side with these texts, which are, however, not very numerous—we find others that could have been composed only by a people that had more or less settled down to an agricultural life; while there are other texts again, that give us a vivid picture of a people who had, to a very large extent, attained a civilised state, who lived in cities, built stone structures, possessed horses and elephants, and used them in their wars, who rode and fought on chariots, and adorned their persons with gold and silver ornaments, who had developed laws and institutions of a comparatively advanced type for their social and civic government. All these records could not belong, surely, to one and the same period of the life of the Vedic Hindus, nor mark, in any way, one single epoch or stage of their social or mental growth. Even there is a marked evolution in their religious ideas as between, for instance, the first and the tenth Mandala of the Rig-Veda,—a gradual growth from a particularistic and naturalistic to a kind of universal and monotheistic * idea of the godhead,—as seen in the well-known text †. The one truth, the Brahmins call by various names, such as, Indra, Varuna, Gadutmat, Rudra &c. It is not at all reasonable, therefore, to treat this varied collection, even of the Sanhita texts, as marking one stage of Hindu evolution. The growth of these texts,—from these that are undoubtedly representative of the earliest known period of Indo-Aryan evolution to those as in the tenth Mandala of the Rig-Veda, for instance, that indicates one advanced synthesis,—could not by any means be accounted by the five hundred years that Professor Max Muller gives as the outside limit for their growth in such an absolutely arbitrary and summary fashion. Professor Balgangadhar Tilak basing his calculations upon astrono-

* Prof. Max Muller would call it not Mono-theistic but Heno-theistic.

† Ekam sad bipra bahudha badanti etc.

mical and geological evidence, the truth of which would be more difficult to contest,—would give as many millenniums and something more also, to measure the growth of the existing Vedic texts, as Prof Max Muller gave centuries. And how can we then take the Vedic Sanhitas, not to mention the other branches of the Vedic literature, as representative of one single stage or moment of Hindu evolution?

And the same remark applies to the Upanishads also. Not to take cognizance of those Upanishabs, like the Gopal-Tapini and others, that are of an obviously modern, or what, at any rate, may be boldly called the post-Pauranic period of Hindu history,—even those that have been accepted as canonical by ancient commentators, do not bear proofs of an absolutely single stage of thought and speculation. It is clear that some of these belong to later, like, for instance, the *Swatasswatara* and to a much earlier period. Professor Max Muller gives 200 years as the probable period of the growth of the Upanishads, and here also his conclusion is unsupported by any valid evidence. But even two hundred years may, under certain circumstances, be not a very insignificant period of a nation's life and history, and they may work, as we know from our own times, mighty changes in the thought and life of a people, such as can never be brought together under one single step or stage or moment of their evolution.

How can we class all the Upanishads together then? And there are distinct evidence of violent conflicts of thoughts and strivings after a settlement and solution of these, in the canonical Upanishads themselves, as we shall see in detail when considering their contributions to Hindu evolution. In some, for instance, the earlier ritualism of the Vedas is absolutely condemned, marking a distinct period of Antethesis. In others, which evidently mark what may be called a stage of Synthesis, there is a clear attempt to work out some settlement, some compromise, some *via media* between the way of knowledge or *Brahmajnana* and the way of works and rituals, or *Karma*. Indeed, it is impossible to study the Upanishads without marking in them a long and laborious course of conflicts and settlements, of progress and evolution. And like the Upanishads, the Puranas also are many, and the so-called Pauranic Hinduism, with its exuberance of symbolism and ceremonialism, is not as some people seem to think, a pathological development of Hindu thought and theology,—but mark a distinct advance upon those of the Vedas and Upanishads, and cover not only a long period but many courses of real progress and evolution. And finally, are we to understand that all progress in Hinduism ceased with the last of the canonical eighteen Puranas? Some of the Tantras are of later date. And what about the successive commentaries of these Puranas by sectarian thinkers and propagandists? What about the comparatively modern movements, and more particularly the Bhakti-movements, or the movements of Love and Faith, both Vaishnavite and Saivite, in Northern as well as Southern India? These are pertinent questions and they tend to show that even modern Hinduism is not a fossil, is not an object-lesson in religious degeneration,—but still a living, growing, changing, expanding, evolving thing. And of a living thing or thought it is impossible to mark, except in a very arbitrary and unscientific way, definite and limited stages of evolution. We can trace the history of a living organism, and this history will necessarily indicate the different moments of its evolution, but there is no warrant whatever, to fix these moments down to any definite number. *

---

§ 3 Prof. Caird's Stages of Religious Evolution Critically Examined.

This characterisation of the earliest phase of human beliefs as known to us, is, in one sense, true; but the term "Object" is essentially a philosophic term implying relation to a Subject, and as suggesting any differentiation in consciousness, between the Self and the not-Self, which this term does

* Caird s Evolution of religion.

> Professor Caird calls the first of the three stages through which religion evolves,—the objective stage; and the essential characteristic of this stage is that man here regards God "as an object among other objects."

seem to imply. Objective would seem to mean surely, a good deal more, when applied to the earliest phase of man's God-idea, than is justified by facts. In the first place, any form whatever of a God-idea, is not a universal feature of the earliest phase of human religion known to primitive culture. There are tribes among whom religion appears in the form of a common and social custom alone. Leaving these cases aside, even where religion, as understood by us is discovered as a specific fact or institution, the word Objective would hardly express adequately the central idea of it. Man in the objective stage, according to Professor Caird, looks upon himself "as an object among other objects," and he conceived his God also as such. But is this analysis of the idea of himself of the primitive man strictly accurate? Has he really any concepts? He forms, no doubt, some generalisations. Without some such generalisations there could hardly be any association of ideas and without such association of ideas there could be no memory. But even lower animals have memory, which also must possess some background of generalisations behind even mere animal intelligence. If these rudimentary generalisations could be called concepts, primitive man may claim to have them, but he has them only in common with the higher orders of the animal kingdom. But the concepts that are generally recognised by us as such, are, however, more advanced and organised forms of thought. They are the fruits of reflection, and the earliest stage of primitive human intelligence can hardly be called reflective. It would hardly be correct, therefore, it seems to us, to say that at that stage man either knows himself as an object, or that he knows any other thing as such. The truth is that in this stage man knows himself really and absolutely as his body—as tall, or short, lean, or fat, white, or black, strong, or week, hungry, or full, happy, or miserable, or as moved or calm, as safe or frightened and so on, and this is about all that he knows or feels of himself directly. To this he adds also some indirect knowledge of himself, derived from others, as having been born of such and such parents, and belonging to such and such family or tribe, and having, as such, certain social obligations. This is all that primitive man, in the earliest known state of his mental evolution, really knows of himself. And this, surely, is not knowing himself as "an object among other objects," unless the expression is taken to mean simply that man at this stage knows himself, just as he knows the things about him—only through his senses—by means of his perceptions and such crude generalisations as are common to all intelligence, animal or human. *Our* analysis of his experiences, in the light of *our own* advanced thought and philosophy, which out of the implications of his immature mind, does present him in the shape in which Prof. Caird describes him. *We* see that all the while primitive man was looking upon himself as an object among other objects, but he did not exactly see himself in this light. He approached himself as much as he approached everything else, simply through the gates of his senses. That seems to us to be the real truth. And whatever distinction he made between himself and others was simply a distinction of me and not-me; and not in any sense of Self and not-Self or of knower and known or Subject and Object. And Prof. Caird's terminology seems, therefore, to us to be open to considerable misconception, and we would prefer to call the earliest phase of the evolution of religion as the Perceptive or, following Prof. Max Muller, the "Naturalistic" state, using the term naturalistic in the sense of unreflective, in which the words "nature" and "natural" are not infrequently used in common parlance.

But the reading of advanced philosophical ideas and intentions into the history of religious evolution is patent throughout Prof. Caird's study of this subject. As he calls the first stage of religious evolution the objective stage, so he calls the second stage the subjective stage, and the third or last stage he characterises as the universal stage. In some religions there is a phase which may very properly be called subjective, but in *some* religions only; and even in these, it would not be possible to prove, we are afraid, that this is the *second* stage in their evolution. But we do not see this strictly subjective phase in all religions, because, owing to difference in race-characteristics, the religious sentiment had not everywhere the same original spiritual sense to work upon, by which alone could a strictly subjective character be developed in any religion. The particular phase of Hinduism represented by some of the ancient Upanishads may well be called subjective, we admit. For in the religion of these Upanishads there is a distinct and preponderating emphasis on the subjective to the more or less entire neglect or denial of the objective. Here the subject is constantly set up over against the object, and practically while all reality is appropriated by the former, the latter is relegated to the realm almost of dreams and shadows. The subject or the Self is the Truth, the object or the not-self is untruth. The subject is everlasting and eternal, the object everchanging and ephemeral. The subject is the reality, the

(b) What Prof. Caird calls the subjective stage, coming after his objective and first stage, can never be said to be common to all systems of religion. A clearly marked stage of religious progress which can properly be called subjective can only be found in the Upanishads.

object is mere appearance. The subject is absolutely independent of and different from the object. It is pure being. This is the keynote of these Upanishads. No one can read through these Hindu scriptures without being impressed with their intense, their excessive and exclusive subjectivity. And coming to these studies after those of the naturalistic poetry and ceremonialism of Vedic religion, this subjectivism of the Upanishads does seem to mark a fresh phase, if not a new stage, in the evolution of Hindu religion. The same thing, though in a much less accentuated form, is also marked, to some extent, in the evolution of the

It may not be quite foreign to the ancient religion of Greece.

ancient religion of Greece, which also bears evidence of a phase of naturalism prior to the philosophic speculations of the later sages and seers. And if all religions were like those of Greece or India, Professor Caird's classification would have some justification. But all religions are not alike, have not had the same original endowments, nor the same historic setting. We do find a subjective phase in Aryan religious evolution, it is true. But do we find it clearly marked in the evolution of the non-Aryan systems? Is there any trace of a truly subjective phase in the history of Judaism? The characteristic of the subjective phase—Prof. Caird's subjective stage—as described by himself is that here God is apprehended as the subject, and as such stands eternally apart from all objects.

But one would search the Old Testament in vain for a corresponding stage.

But where do we find God apprehended thus in the Old Testament records? When and where? There is an objective, or as we would prefer to call, a perceptive phase in Judaism, as we shall see later on. There is a later phase where God is apprehended as a Super-sensuous Being, but at no time was he apprehended really as the subject by the ancient Hebrews. The God of Judaism is super-sensuous, but super-sensuousness is not the only, nor an absolutely essential characteristic of what is called the subject in philosophy. He is omniscient but even omniscience does not directly and necessarily cancel all objectivity. Either we must accept the term subjective in a much looser sense than is admitted in philosophical literature, or we must confess that even an Omniscient being is not necessarily *the* Subject or the Absolute. We are all subjects in relation to our objects: we are also objects in relation to other selfs or subjects. Our being a Subject does not preclude,—except at the final analysis of the concept subject which leads to absolute monism—our being also at the same time objects. God may similarly be omniscient and may have the whole creation for his object, and yet, in as much as he becomes an *object* of our knowledge, he too becomes to us an object. When, therefore,

God, whether He be seen or unseen, finite or infinite, becomes an object of man's knowledge, the religion which apprehends and presents him as such, becomes objective. And mere omniscience or omnipotence or any other attributes ascribed to the Deity in such a religion would not lend to it, what Prof. Caird calls, a subjective phase.

In the entire range of human religions, so far as it is known to us, the religion of the Upanishads alone can claim really to present a truly subjective phase. Because there is absolutely no suspicion of any objectivity in the Upanishadic conception of the Deity. The Upanishads distinctly say that the Supreme knows everything but of Him there is no knower. And thus they cut off the very roots of all objective ideas concerning the Godhead. Is he then absolutely unknown and unknowable? Yes, reply the Upanishads without any doubt or hesitancy. *

The Upanishads alone distinctly say that there is no knower of the Supreme who knows everything.

न तत्र चक्षुर्गच्छति न वाग् गच्छति नो मनो
न विद्मो न विजानीमो यथैतदनुशिष्यात्।
अन्यदेव तद्विदितादथो अविदितादधि
इति शुश्रुमः पूर्व्वेषां ये नस्तद् व्याचचक्षिरे॥

"The eye does not go there (*i. e.* to Brahman),

* Kena Upanishad I. 3.

the speech does not go there, neither does the mind or the understanding. We do not know it. We know not how to impart instruction about it. It is distinct from what is known, it is beyond what is unknown; this is what we have heard from former teachers who have explained it to us."

But this nescience is not the final teaching of these scriptures. All that it means is that Brahman is unknown and unknowable *as an object.* But Brahman is known and knowable as *subject*, known and knowable, that is,—not as the *known* but as *knower.* We know Brahman just as we know ourselves. Those who know their own Self know Brahman, for the Self and Brahman are one. This, briefly, is the real subjectivism of the Upanishads. This is the true subjective conception of the Deity. Every other conception of God as an object of our knowledge, is distinctly objective. This Upanishadic phase of Hinduism is the only strictly subjective phase of religious evolution we know of in the entire range of the existing religious records of humanity. Do we find it as the second stage,—if we find it at all, in the evolution of the other world-religions? Are there proofs of this phase in Judaism? Are there traces of it in Islam, except in the teachings and experiences of those who have been condemned as heretics? Had this stage been

It means that the *Brahman* is unknown and unknowable as an object though known and knowable as subject.

reached at any time by Latin Christianity? And if there are no proofs of this, the only true subjective phase or stage of religious evolution in so many of the grown-up religions of humanity, how can we follow Professor Caird and accept it as a universal moment in the evolution of man's religion?

The third and last stage of religious evolution is characterised by Prof. Caird as the Universal stage. In this stage, the conflict between the subject and the object that marked the second or the subjective stage, is overcome by the consciousness of an essential unity between the two. The Subject and Object are both here apprehended as moments or phases of the Absolute, which cancels this differentiation between them immediately it is formulated. And thus, Prof. Caird reaches, in this the last and highest phase or stage of religious evolution, the philosophy of Absolute Idealism of which he is one of the ablest exponents in England. Logically his scheme of religious evolution is correct, because it represents, as we have already pointed out, the dialectic of Reason, the universal procession of thought and knowledge. But the confusion in this presentation arises out of its application to actual religious history. For as we

(c) The last stage which Prof. Caird calls the absolute stage—the stage of Synthesis of the dialectic ofReason—is also found only in the later Upanishads and the Puranas and Bhakti Sastras in any thing like an explicit and developed form.

have, no doubt, a truly subjective phase in Hindu evolution, in the religion of the earlier Upanishads, so we do find a truly universal phase also in the later Upanishads, and, as we shall see in course of our investigations, in a more developed form, in the religion of the Puranas, especially in the philosophy and religion of the Hindu Schools of Love and Faith,—both Vaishnavite and Saivite. But do we find any traces of this universal phase in any other world-religion? Not to speak of Judaism or Islam, do we find it even in Christianity, except in the life and experiences of solitary saints and sages,—and these generally belong to the Catholic Church,—in whom what may be called, the Christ-consciousness assumed a universal form, cancelling all conflicts if not all differentiations, and revealing itself through all creation; as well as, in a feeble though extremely pregnant note in the philosophy and culture of the Alexandrian Fathers, and also in that form of philosophical Christianity which has come to be associated with the name of Hegel, the new school of Christian Theology to which Prof. Caird himself belongs?

Judaism and Islam can not claim any such Stages. Even in Christianity it is realised only in certain solitary individuals, Sects and Schools.

It seems to us, indeed, that the scheme of the evolution of Religion, presented by Professor Caird is somewhat arbitrary and subjective. He marks three stages of this Evolution. But why *three* at all? The dialectic of Reason suggests no doubt three logical stages of evolution, but can we apply it chronologically to any particular history of religious evolution? Thesis, antethesis, and synthesis, or homogeneity, differentiation, and integration, these do represent the logic of the evolutionary process. But in actual course of evolution do not these follow one another very rapidly, and is not the circle repeated almost endlessly in the history of every form of psychological evolution? In thought or reason, thesis, antethesis and synthesis do not appear, at any time, in what may be characterised as a static or stationary aspect. They form an ever-recurring circle. Thesis, antethesis and synthesis represent, so to say, the dynamics of reason or thought. The whole process is in perpetual motion. Thesis as soon as formulated, commences to create its own antethesis, which also immediately sets in motion its own synthesis. The logical process of evolution is really, as we have said, a process of what Christian theologians call, eternal generation. And in evolution, whether biological or psychological, it is absolutely impossible to say where one stage ends and another begins, and consequently we cannot, as a matter of fact

Chronologically speaking, Prof Card's presentaton is, therefore, arbitrary and subjective. The moments of the dialetic of Reason ever repeated in the process of Evolution, represent the dynamic aspect of it—a process of eternal gengation of which the moments are practically inseparable

divide these stages at all. All such division must be merely theoretic, abstract, and arbitrary ; and at best it can only be logically but never chronologically true.

CHAPTER IV.

The Source of Religion

§ 1. Max Muller's Theory of its Origin

Modern investigations trace the origin of religion in nature worship or ancester worship—Miller and Spencer

Philosophy of Religion, or what Max Muller preferred to call the Science of Religion, as far as it has been investigated and worked up, traces the origin of the religious phenomena either in nature-worship or in ancestor-worship. Hume, and following him, Herbert Spencer, attribute the birth of religion to anestor-worship. Max Muller, on the other hand, has sought to trace the origin of man's religious consciousness to his intuitions of the Infinite within and his contact with and contemplation of the natural forces and phenomena without, which acted as the first stimuli to quicken his inner intuitions of the Infinite. But both Spencer and Max Muller seem to us to present only a half-truth. Prof Max Muller defines religion as the sense of the infinite in man. * But what is this infinite? He could not, consistently, claim that his theory of religious evolution was a *science*,

Max Muller rather inconsistently calls his work a science as his source—the idea of the Infinite—is beyoud the Scope of Science.

* For the exact terms. Vide Scicnce of Religion.

when he presented an abstruse philosophical term as expressing the very essence and substance of the phenomena which he undertook to investigate. Science goes no further than the indefinite: it knows no infinity. The highest point in mathematics, for instance, though for courtesy's sake called an infinity, is really not infinite but simply indefinite. If it can at all be called an infinity, it is what may be called a spatial infinite, which, every student of metaphysics knows, is no infinity at all, but is only another name for that which the vision of man cannot comprehend, and in thinking of which the mind of man loses itself in immensity. But true infinity is not realisable by the eye, but by the self, the spirit, which itself is infinite. The Absolute alone is Infinite, and not science but philosophy or metaphysics alone can reveal the Absolute to us.

He, perhaps, refers to the intuition of the Absolute and Infinite, rather, the vague sense of the Unknown, present throughout the whole process of religious Evolution, as the back ground of all.

But though the ultimate meaning and truth of the Infinite or Absolute can only be realised and attained by deep abstraction and great mental and moral excellence, the result of long and laborious training and disciplines, there is, yet, it must be admitted, a general and vague feeling or intuition of it in every man. Man's affinites with, his longing for, his groping after the Absolute does constitute, therefore, the universal back-ground of his religious life and experiences, and this vague sense of the Unknown, if not really of the Infinite, is present at every step of the evolution of human religion from the lowest to the highest. And in this sense Prof. Max Muller's definition is capable of defence. But where it fails is in its interpretations of the Infinite, as *actually* apprehended by the primitive mind. The sense of the Infinite is intuitional.

But his limitation consists in the position that this sense of the Infinite is quickened by Nature above.

But every intuition needs external and objective stimuli to be quickened into activity and consciousness. What is the objective and external stimulus that, acting upon the mind of man, first quickened, however feebly it might be, his intuitions of the Infinite, and thus gave birth to his religion? It is Nature, says Professor Max Muller. The "infinitely large" and the "infinitely small" things and objects about him quickened man's earliest intuitions of the Infinite. The sky, foremost of all; broad expanse of plains, sometimes; lofty mountains; meandering rivers losing themselves in unknown realms and coming also from unprospected regions;—the sea, the forest, the phenomena of light and darkness;—these and similar natural objects and phenomena aroused men's sense of the Infinite. This is Prof. Max Muller's view. It is partly true also. But only partly, and its lack of fullness is a fatal limitation. A definition must cover, and an explanation must meet, the whole field and every phase of its object. Professor Max Muller's fails in this. The Nature-sense, so to say, had, no doubt, a potent influence in the development of religion among Aryan peoples, but surely not among all peoples. In others

But though nature-note is prominent in early Hinduism, the influence of Social organism is prominent among the Chinese.

the primary emphasis is not on man's contact with his Nature-surroundings, but rather on his relations with the social organism to which he belongs. Among the Chinese, for instance, Nature is approached through the prism of the social experience, and interpreted in the terms of the Social life. The head of the social life, the Emperor, is also the head of the life of Nature, and he used to issue edicts deposing the heavenly bodies just as he did in regard to his earthly mandarins. To trace the origin of the religious sentiment, therefore, to man's sense of Infinity as quickned by contact with his Nature-surroundings, would fail to meet the case of the Chinese, and to some extent, perhaps, even of the Semitic races, with whom also the social sense seems to have dominated over what may be called the Nature-sense. The religion of Israel is called covenantal religion; it owed its origin to a covenant or contract between the God and the people of Israel. In the Old Testament the expression Lord of Hosts means in the earlier stages, simply the Commander of the Army of Israel,—an idea fully supported by the theoratic form of the social and civic government of the early Jews. It is only subsequently that the celestial army of stars and planets came to be included in the "hosts" of the Lord. And this shows very clearly the social emphasis of Judaism, in the entire literature of which the Nature-note is exceedingly feeble and subordinate. Had Professor Max Muller applied his theory of the origin of the religious sense, to the religious history of the Chinese, or even to the history of the Old Testament religion, he would, we are sure, have himself discovered the fatal limitations under which it laboured, and for which his interpretations of the phenomena of human religions have failed to some extent.

And the Jews,

The fact, really, is that what Prof. Max Muller calls, in a somewhat loose way, the sense of the Infinite, is only a consciouness of what may be called the "Not-Me." This "Not-Me" is what man comes to feel first of all, surrounding him on all sides,—opposing him sometimes, and, perhaps helping and befriending him at other. The so-called Infinite of Prof. Max Muller is only this "Not-Me" of the primitive man, and it would be absolutely correct to say that man's religion grows always and everywhere out of his contact and conflict with this "Not-me". What

Max Muller's "Infinite" and Caird's 'object' mean, perhaps, the 'not-me' which surrounds the primitive man on all sides and out of contact and conflict with which his religion grows. ——It is the *Idam* as contrasted with *Aham*.

Prof. Caird characterises as "object," is only this "Not-me". Others have called the earliest phase of religious evolution, as particularistic, instead of objective. But like Prof. Cairds "objects," their "particular" are also found, at the final analysis to be only forms of the "Not-me,"—what in Hindu Philosophy is characterised by the general term *Idam* or this, that is, what is not *Aham* or I or me.

But this is speaking in the terms, it may be said, of the unknown, what in mathemetics is called X and Y, the "not-me" is an unknown quantity, and may mean, therefore, as much or as little, as Prof. Max Muller's "Infinite." No, by no means so. For this "not-me" is a very tangible thing to primitive man. It is the Power-not-Himself that constantly curbs and controls him. In his nature-surroundings the primitive man stands perpetually face to face with a power-not-Himself that curbs and controls his activities. He sees it in the roaring thunder, in the rushing storm-wind, in world-devouring forest-fires, in running volumes of water, in cataclysms like earth-quakes and tarnadoes, as well as, at a later stage, in the movements of the heavenly bodies, and the mysterious play of light and darkness at nights, and at dawn and even-tide. All these are his "Not-Me," represent powers and personalities to him that have a hold upon his life

It is the Power-not-Himself that constantly curbs and controls man in his activities.

and that can make or mar his happiness at their will. This perception of the Not-Me in nature is the origin, really, of all nature-deities whether found in the ancient records of the Hindus or the Greeks or of any other race. All the mere prominent Vedic gods, like most of the earlier Hellenic deities, belong to this class. And it is, evidently, a consideration of these that had led Prof. Max Muller to attribute the earliest quickening of man's intuitions of the Infinite to his contact with and contemplation of the awful mysteries of Nature.

The nature deities of the early Greeks and the Hindus originate from the perception of the "Not-Me" in nature. Max Miller's conclusion is a hasty generalisation from this fact.

---

§ 2. Hume and Spencer's Theory

Nature, however, is not the only aspect in which the "Not-Me" or the "Power-not-Himself" that sought to control man, stood face to face with him, in the earliest state of his existence. As in his Nature-surroundings primitive man saw and felt the presence of a Power-not-Himself that stood in opposition to his desires and activities, so also in his social life, in the authority of his tribe, in the rites and customs enjoined upon him by tribal law and tradition, that had behind them the sanction of his ancestors, primitive man became, at every step, conscious of a controlling and awful outside agency. While Max Muller saw, from his study, specially, of the primitive records of the Aryan religions this Power-not-Himself that quickened man's earliest consciousness of religion, in his nature-surroundings, Hume and Herbert Spencer, from their special examination of the records of the life and thought of savage man, as found in books of travels, saw this Power-not-Himself only in the social authority and traditions of primitive man, and the one took nature-worship as the first expression of human religions while the two others took ancestor-worship to represent that earliest phase. The fact, however, is that the earliest phase of religious evolution testifies to the presence of a dual force acting upon the instincts of man, one, what may be called the Nature force, giving rise to the worship of what has been called Nature deities, such as are found in early Hindu and Hellenic religion, the other, social force, which led to the worship of ancestors, as the source, the sanction, and the fountain-head of it. Out of this dual consciousness of a Power-not-Himself,—that manifested in Nature-phenomena and in social authority,—man's earliest religion seems to have grown up.

But the primitive man found himself controlled also by social authority and traditions. Hume and Spencer seem to generalise from cases illustrating this fact in tracing this source of religion in ancester worship.

Man's earliest religion, the product of a dual force —nature and society.

§ 3. Man's earliest Religion product of both Elements

Indeed, as Nature formed an essential factor in the life of man, so did also Society, at every stage of its growth. His nature environments have been as constant a factor of his evolution as his social-environments. We know of no time, in the history of man, when he did not live in, and form part of, some social organisation. It is his relation, organic almost, and pre-historic, with other men and women, forming members of one and the same community or tribe, speaking the same dialect, observing the same customs, tracing a common origin, that really differentiate man even in the most primitive state from every other species of animal, We can conceive of no time when man was not a social being, and even pre-historic research furnish no evidence of such a period of human evolution. And this social bond has universally constituted an essential element of his religion. In fact where we find absolutely no idea of a god-head, no injunctions regarding worship, no records, direct or in-direct, of any instinct or sense that might be referred to the Unseen, where, in short, we find no trace of what is usually known to and understood by us as religion, even there we find this obedience to social authority, in the form of observance of

Both the factors essential and constant.

social customs, as the only substitute for religion. But his social environments supplied only one-half of man's religious incentive, the other half was supplied by his natural or physical environments.

Though there are considerable variations in the emphasis on them in the different systems:

And these two, Nature and Society, constituted always the two agencies that worked up, everywhere, the religious consciousness of mankind. But there has been considerable variations in the emphasis that has been laid on these two essential stimuli and vehicles of man's religious-ideas. In some people, the emphasis has been on Nature, in others on Society, while in some, again, it has been fairly divided between them two where the emphasis has been stronger on the Social than on the Nature environments, as it seems to have been, for instance among the Chinese,

(*a*) Among the Chinese and the Hebrews the stronger social factor interprets the nature-forces in its own terms.

and, in another fashion, among also the Hebrews as well, there, Nature-forces have been viewed and expressed in the terms of the social life and relations,—the conception of a social hierarchy rising, in gradation, from family-authority, represented by the worship of ancestors, to the imperial authority, represented by the Sovereign, the earthly manifestation and instrument of the Royal-dead, is transferred also to the Government and organisation of the physical world, as we see in China ; or the conception of an earthly theocracy is transferred to represent a similar rule in Nature, and the hosts of Yahveh represent an earthly army here, and an army of stars and planets above, as we find in the records of the children of Israel. Among the Aryans, however, this emphasis has been, it seems, very fairly divided from the earliest times, between the Nature-forces and the social-authority, and we find in the Vedas a dual religion, so to say, one consisting of the worship of Nature-deities and the other that of ancestors, and these two lines of religious sacraments and duties run parallel to each other throughout the entire course of the evolution of early Vedic Hinduism. And even in subsequent evolution, as the Nature-deities gradually united and coalesced, so to say, in the conception of Brahman, the One Ttuth—the *Ekam Sat*, as it is put in the tenth Mandala of the Rig Veda, so the social deities, the ancestral spirits, also united and coalesced in that of Prajapati, Brahman represented the highest synthesis, in the pre-Upanishadic stage, of the Nature-Gods while Prajapati represented that of the social Gods or ancestral spirits ; and Brahman and Prajapati, like the Devas and the Pitris, divided Vedic worship equally between them, for a very long

(*b*) But among the early Vedic Hindus the emphasis was fairly divided between the two.

In a higher stage of Evolution the nature-deities gradually united and coalesced in the conception of *Brahman* and the social-deities synthesised in the notion of *Prajapati.*

period, it seems, of the evolution of primitive Hinduism. And even when it reached the stage of monotheism, the social-emphasis was not entirely lost, but Prajapati was still retained, as we shall see later on, in the conception of Hiranyagarbha, the first born of Brahman, the origin of social life and order, the first teacher of truths, the first promulgator of Law.

In the highest synthesis of monotheism, the conception of Hiranya—Garbha contains social-emphasis.

But Society forms *one* essential element of man's religion. The other essential element has been supplied by his physical environments. In the earliest stage, his mind was naturally absorbed by terrestrial phenomena. He was then engaged in clearing the earth, and making it fit for human habitation. His mind was, naturally, fixed on the earth. At this stage fire must have played a very important part in his life. Primitive man first stood face to face with fire, in its natural manifestation of jungle-fire, —self-produced, forest-devouring, terrible and over-whelming to both man and beast, yet ultimately turning out to be the greatest friend of man, in as much as it cleared the surface of the earth of both beasts and vegetation, opening it out, thus, for human habitation. Fire, therefore, we find in the Vedas, described as the first-born of the gods. In the jungle-

Of the phenomena of nature the celestial succeed the terrestial and those having more direct reference to his daily life precede those that are remote in that respect, in evoking religion consciousness in man.

clearing stage man had, really, no leisure to contemplate the majestic sweep of the heavens. He was then too absorbingly engaged in fighting his terrestrial enemies, and overcoming the obstacles that Mother Earth raised before him, to indulge in pleasant dreams of the Sun and the Moon, or the brilliants of the blue vault above him. Celestial phenomena came later to receive his notice, and of these storm and wind, thunder and lightning, must have received much earlier notice. The heavens as the panorama of light and darkness or as a symbol of all-embracing, all-pervading immensity, which Max Muller calls the symbol of the Infinite, entered much later into man's reflections, to form, thus, an element of his religion or a vehicle of his worship. But natural objects and phenomena, whether terrestrial or celestial, supplied always, at every stage, and everywhere, one aspect of the great *Not-Me*, through which man first commenced to feel after his Maker, while his Society formed the other aspect of it. And the truth, about the origin of the religious sentiment, does not lie, therefore, either in the theory of Hume or Spencer on the one side, nor in that of Max Muller, on the other, but partly in both; the full truth being found in the combination of the two. For man's religion has always been an attempt on his part to adjust himself to his nature-surroundings on the one

Religion is thus an attempt at adjustment to natural and social environment.

side, and to his social-surroundings on the other.

It is the harmony of the individual with his environments and, in a higher stage, the harmony of the inner self to the outer life.

Religion may, therefore, be defined, with the Greeks, as Harmony: the harmony of the individual man with his environments in every aspect and department of his life and activities, as well as, in the higher and more spiritual stages, harmony also with his inner self—his inner ideas, ideals, desires, aspirations, and cravings, and his outer life and activities and the social and civic institutions in and through which that life and those activities find their instrument and fulfilment. And the true History of Religion is only the history of the attempt that man has always made, with varying success, to adjust himself to his physical, his mental, his moral or social, his civic and economic conditions, and, through this progressive adjustment, to develop the highest possibilities of his nature, and realise the loftiest promise of his soul.

History of Religion is the history of such a progressive adjustment or harmony of the self to the various conditions of life for its highest realisation.

This, it seems to us, is the view of religion, in its most general aspect that a comparative study of the religious experiences of humanity most fully supports. It supplies a key by which almost every religion may be unlocked,—from what is called the lowest forms of animism, fetishism, or totemism, to the highest forms of monotheism or theosophy or gnosticism, whether Hindu or Christian or Islamic.

This is the view of religion most consistent with the comparative Study of the wide religious experiences of humanity.

CHAPTER V.

Evolution of Religion.

§ 1. It Evolves with the Evolution of the Views of Self and not-Self.

Religious life grows with the growth of man's contact with nature and society and the consequent increase of his knowledge of them.

Contact with the "*Not Me*" in its dual aspect of Nature-force and Social-Authority, is the originating cause, then, of the religious consciousness in man. It grows and expands, necessarily, with the growth and expansion of this contact, and the consequent advancement in man's knowledge and ideas concerning his natural and his social life and limitations. All differences between one religion and another is explicable by the different estimates that man has formed in different countries and at different times of these two aspects of his Not-Me, as well as by the difference of the emphasis that has been laid, by different peoples, on one or other of these dual factors of their life. The study of these variations, as well as of the fundamental unity underlying them all, with a view to work out the general laws and principles involved in the origin and growth of human religions, is the object of what may be called the Science or Philosophy of Religion. And, as we have already said, the

Science or philosophy of Religion is the study of the variations as well as of the underlying unity of the different estimates of the two aspects of the "Not Me" in different countries and by different peoples, by critical observation and proper application of the histrio-comparative method.

methods of investigation here are the common methods of Science, namely, observation, experiment, comparison, classification and generalisation, to which must be added the two most important methods of investigating living and growing objects and institutions, namely, the comparative and the historic method, corrected, verified, and illumined by the general law of psychological or mental evolution.

Religion being, thus, in its broadest and most universal sense, the attempt of man to adjust himself to his "*Not Me*," with a view to the realisation of his own highest end, the evolution of religion must, necessarily, follow the course of relationship in which man enters, in his progress through life, with this *Not-Me*. And, indeed, we find it always in actual history that man's religion has always changed or advanced in accordance with his progressive or changing views of this *Not-Me*, as his views of this *Not-Me* also have, themselves, changed and evolved, in accordance with man's changing and advancing views of himself.

Evolution of Religion Corresponds to the Evolution of man's view of the "Not-Me" which, again, Corresponds to the Evolution of his view of himself.

Man's relations with his *Not-Me* are of three classes. The *Not-Me* is, in the first place, an object of man's knowledge. All his senses operate on and through this *Not-Me*. He sees it, he smells it, he hears it, he touches it, he tastes it,—in Nature, and he feels its presence and power in his relations with it, in his social life. By these means he comes to know of the *Not-Me.* Man here is, though he may not always know it himself,—what we would with our advanced knowledge call, the knower of the *Not-Me*, the *Not-Me* is the object of his knowledge :- he is the subject, the Not-Me is his object. This is one relation. And it is the character of every relation that any changes in one of the factors of it, brings on a change necessarily in the other factor also, so far as the particular relation is concerned. Consequently man's views of himself have always changed with his altered views concerning his Not-Me; as his changed views in regard to the Not-Me have also changed similarly his own estimates and ideas concerning his own self.

(a) This is due, in the first place, to the relation of the knower and the known between the self and the not-self.

Change in man's nature-surroundings owing to his migration to a different and distant region of the earth is a real change in his *Not-Me.* So also is what contact with an alien social organisation must necessarily work in the other, the social aspect of his *Not-Me.* And these changes have contributed very largely to very distinct changes in man's religious ideas and ideals where even the original religion seems to have been one. Differences between Judaism and Islam are of this class and character, as well as the

Illustrated in the changes in religion owing to migration and contact with alien social organisation.

differentiations that are observed in the religions of ancient India and ancient Greece. In the one case these were brought about by the dispersion of the Semitic, in the other by that of the Aryan race.

(b) Secondly, it is due to the relation of the enjoyer and enjoyed between them.

As the *Not-Me* stands to man in the relation of known to knower, or object to subject, so also it stands to him in that of enjoyer and enjoyed. Man not only knows the Not-Me through his perceptions, but every act of perception calls up sensations of either pleasure or pain, and thus, man, stands perpetually related to the Not-Me through his sensations or feelings. And here also, progressively to man's capacity to *feel*, as well as to the *Not-Me's* power or opportunity to *make* him feel, his relations with it must change, and such changes must necessarily lead to important developments in his religious ideas and ideals.

(c) Thirdly, it is due to the relation of the agent and the object of action between them.

And, finally, the *Not-Me* is not only an object of man's knowledge or of his emotions,—is not something that he perceives by his senses, or something that causes him pleasure or pain, fills him with admiration or disgust, or awe or contempt,—something that works upon his emotions, but it is also something that calls forth his energies and impels him to some form or other of activity always. In our present state, there may be things that we perceive about us but which neither draw nor repel us. In these cases perceptions do not evoke emotion, and in the absence of emotion, the will is not moved. But this is largely, if not wholly, due to the comparatively higher stage of mental evolution that we have reached. In this matter, the adult man or woman in civilisation differs very much from little children whose perceptions are uniformly associated with sensation and volition. It is universally observed in babies. Savages, not trained to habits of reflection, are like babies in this respect, and the necessary relation between perception, sensation and will-movement is proved more clearly in their life than in ours. But the Not-Me is to us, as it is to them, equally subject to the operation of the will. Man knows the *Not-Me*, and stands to it in the relation of subject to object. He feels the Not-Me and stands to it in the relation of feeler and felt,—or as we have in Sanskrit, enjoyer and enjoyed—भोग्य भोक्तारम—*Bhogya-Bhaktaram.* He is moved to action by the Not-Me, and stands to it, thus in the relation of agent to the object of his activity.

The actualities of this three-fold relation, then, determine the course of Evolution of religion.

And the course of evolution in religion is determined by the actualities of this triune-relation in which man stands always to his Not-Me, as represented by his Nature-environment, and his Social organism, the changes in this triune-relation accounting for his changing ideas both of his Deity and his Duty.

---

§ 2. Its Psychological Process.

The process of such an Evolution is clearly a psychological phenomenon and should be studied as such.

The course of religious evolution must, therefore, be studied as an essentially psychological phenomenon. It must be studied, that is, in the light of the evolution of human reason, human emotions, and the human will. The earliest stage in this psychological evolution must mark the earliest stage also of religious evolution, and so on the two courses of evolution must, necessarily, advance along parallel lines.

In the earliest stage of mental evolution we find three things, namely, (1) Perception of sense-objects (2) Sensations of pleasure and pain, and (3) Activity to attain the one and avoid the other. This is, in most general terms, child psychology. This is also, more or less, the psychology of primitive man, in the earliest stage. This is what may be called the naturalistic stage of human culture.

(A) Its Naturalistic or Perceptive Stage.

Man here is not but little removed from the brute creation. His senses are his main guides in life. Instinct is in possession, here, of his reason. When he reasons at all, as he must necessarily do in taking his experiences of yesterday as a guide for to-day, he does so instinctively, so to say, and not by any conscious, reasoned, process. His experience is limited. His vision is narrow. His generalisations are few, such as are observed in the play of intelligence even in lower animals. His emotions also are of a very simple character. The complexity observed in the thoughts, emotions, and impulses of civilised man is absolutely unknown here. And his activities are also of the simplest, the most direct and crude nature. This is the inventory of the mental life of primitive man. And his religion also is in perfect consonance with this life of perceptions, sensations, instincts and animal impulses ;—perceptions supplying the object of his worship, sensations the motives for it, and instinct and impluse furnishing the methods and appliances, the rites and ceremonies of his worship. This may very properly be called the naturalistic stage or phase of religious evolution.

In the naturalistic stage of religious Evoluton the perceptions, sense-feelings, instincts and impulses of the child man supply the objects, motives and methods of his worship.

And, as we have already said, this term naturalistic, or as we would ourselves prefer to call it, perceptive, would seem to be a more accurate characterisation of the first phase of religious evolution than Prof. Caird's objective, because they follow more closely, perhaps, the dialectic of reason. In the dialetic of Reason, the first or earliest stage is that of unity,—undifferentiated and homogenous unity. But the term objective presupposes differentiation, breaking up, that is, of this homogeneity; for there can be no consciousness, strictly speaking, of an object without that of a subject, which stands over against it. Where the subject is unconscious, there is really and truly no object either. Indeed, the first movement of knowledge is an undifferentiated perception, and mere perception, though it does generate knowledge by differentiating it from other perceptions and putting them on a line, (integrating) with it, does not imply differentiation of subject and object. Indeed, what may be called, in some sense, a pure state of nature, is decidedly a state of homogeneity. In our mental life it is the stage where no distinctions have yet arisen between the knower and known, between subject and object, except that of me and not-me. All knowing in this earliest stage is almost

As this first stage is that of undifierentiated unity, it should more accurately be called 'Naturelistic' or, rather, 'Perceptive' and not 'Objective' which implies differentiation between subject and object.

entirely perceiving, an operation of the senses without much analysis, reflection, or generalisation. It is therefore that we prefer to call the first stage of religious evolution, as the Naturalistic or the Perceptive stage.

(i) The Earliest Stage Essentially Perceptive.

And the actual history of human religions supports this nomenclature. In the earliest stage the senses play a dominant part in the development of the religious sentiment. The Deity here is not really an invisible, supersensuous Being, but are all visible and "sensible" gods and godesses, only though visible, there is always something "uncanny" and mysterious about them, something that suggests hidden powers for good or evil and undiscovered possibilities. And this element of mystery is essential to raise an object or phenomenon, however close and clear it may, otherwise, lie within the range of man's senses, to the position of a thing to be feared, and, therefore, to be worshipped, that is, either conquered or propitiated. But this element

The history of human religions shows that the earliest religion is essentially Perceptive inspite of the element of mystery involved.

of mystery notwithstanding, man's earliest religion, like the earliest phase of his mental life, is essentually one of perceptions. We should like, therefore, to characterise the first and earliest phase of human religion as Perceptive, instead of Objective.

Religion originates, as we have seen, in man's attempt to adjust himself to his Not-Me. This Not-Me presents itself to primitive man always and everywhere in the dual aspect of Nature-Force and Social Authority. And, in the earliest stage, both Nature and Society are viewed by man absolutely through the senses, unassociated with any reflection, except what is essential to the excercise of memory, and what is, consequently, common to all animal intelligence. Even in this stage fundamental differences are observed in the religious ideas and acts of different races. Among some the emphasis as we have said, is more on their social life than on their Nature-environments ; among others it is more on the Nature-environments, perhaps, than on their social life ; while among certain races, from the very beginning, so far as we can see from their most ancient records, this emphasis seems to have been pretty fairly divided between the natural and the social aspects of their Not-Me.

Inspite of all differences, even in this earliest stage, in emphasis on the various aspects, the basis of sense-perception is common to all early stages of religions.

But whatever differences might, thus, be observed even in the earliest phase of their evolution, between different religions, the fact of their being based essentially upon sense-perceptions is common to all. The earliest Vedic deities, Agni, Varuna, the Maruts, Rudra, Indra, the twins Aswini Kumars, are all visible objects. So also are all the oldest Hellenic gods. So also is the earliest God-perception of the Hebrews, inspite of all their claims to a superior and supernatural revelation of divine truths. El-Elohim, translated as Lord Almighty in the English version of the Old Testament, walks the earth, and is visible to his first creatures. Adam and Eve see him, and he sees them, and that this seeing is literal and not metaphorical is proved by their hiding themselves from their creator, and by the creator calling out for them, showing that he could not see them in their hiding, and their answering him from their secret shelter. The entire story is clearly the record of a very human, that is, sensuous drama. Scholars are of opinion, no doubt, that the story of the Fall is not original to the Hebrews, but that they borrowed it from others. But whatever may be its source, the fact is absolutely undeniable that this story in the Book of Genesis represents the perceptive phase of religion, and even the Jews must have had such a phase, as otherwise it would not have been possible for them to adapt it to their traditions. All these are remnants of very old records, no doubt, as all ancient cosmogonies everywhere are, more or less, and there is absolutely no justification for interpreting these passages in the light of our larger experience, in a figurative sense. The Negro who, in obedience to ancient custom, still offers in our own time, food to the tree or the bush that has been worshipped from time immemorial by his ancient forbears may say that the invisible spirit of the tree eats the invisible essence of the offerings, and it is, therefore, that though eaten, the food, apparently remains the same, (1) but still, it is a fact that his primitive ancestors made no distinction, like him, between the tree or bush, as they saw it, and its invisible spirit. Such a consciousness would presuppose the cognition of the self as distinguished from the not-self, a conciousness of the soul or spirit of man as not only differentiated from, but absolutely independent of the body. Yet nowhere, nay not even among people who have had, it seems, an original endowment of a spiritual sense, is this consciousness seen so

And there is no justification for interpreting them in the light of our larger experience, in a figurative sense.

(1) See Tylor's Primitive Culture and Early History of Mankind.

fully developed in primitive culture. The earliest conception—if we may at all apply the term to what was only a perception—of the god-head was nowhere that of an invisible, supersensuous being or thing, but that of something which, though cognisable by the senses, was still shrouded in some profound or awful mystery, either owing to its very nature, or owing to some memories associated, by tradition, with it.

The early conception of God is always sensuous or perceptual though shrouded in awful mystery.

Indeed, not only in the Book of Genesis, but even in Exodus, where we come across the records of a somewhat advanced phase of Judaic religion, we find mention of a "sensible" god-head. Elohim walked the earth at Eden; and was seen and heard with their mortal eye and ear, by Adam and Eve, in the book of Genesis. Yahveh or Jehovah, the new name in which the God of Israel presents himself to Moses, in Exodus, is also seen by him, though somewhat mediately, in, or through, or as, a burning bush. Yahveh talks to Moses even as Elohim had done to Adam. He too is *almost* a visible, and undoubtedly an audible God. Gradually, however, he passes out of both man's sight and hearing. But even long afterwards the tradition is kept up; and the Ark of Shilo becomes

Even the Exodus speaks of a "sensible" godhead showing that the tradition is kept up long even in an advanced stage.

the symbol or nmemonic of the old vision and a whole party of Israelites are punished with immediate death, in verification of the old saying of Yahveh,—"no man shall see God and live" for foolishly, and possibly in a sceptical spirit, prying into the sacred mystery.

(II) The Perceptive Charactor of the God-Experience in early Hebrew Records:—

In fact, the sensuous or perceptive character of the God-experience of the early Hebrew records cannot be denied. In Genesis 3, 8-10. we read .—"And they *heard* the voice of the Lord God *walking* in the garden in the cool of the day; and Adam and his wife *hid themselves* from the presence of the Lord God *amongst the trees* of the garden." (8) "And the Lord God called unto Adam and said unto him, *Where art thou?*" (9)

(I) In Genesis 3.

"And he said, *I heard thy voice* in *the garden*, and I was afraid. *because I was naked* and I hid myself." (10)

And next follows what sounds like an enquiry into the facts of their disobedience: God asks Adam; he refers to Eve; he next asks Eve. who refers to the serpent, and they are all punished.

The same perceptive God-experience is recorded also in Genesis 4, for here also God appears before Abel and Cain, and has a long converse with the latter, and being punished for killing his brother, Cain "went out from the presence of the Lord and dewlt in the land of Nod, on the east of Eden." (verse 16).

(II) In Genesis 4.

In the next place, God *repents* his creation—(Genesis 6. 6 and 7), and sends the flood, but appears before Noah and directs him to make the Ark and go and take shelter in it. After the Deluge, Noah builds an alter unto the Lord, and offers burnt offerings on it. "And the Lord *smelled* a sweet savour; and the Lord said in his heart, I will not again curse the ground any more for man's sake; &c—(8. 21-22)

(iii) In Genesis 6.

The Lord appears before Abraham, however, subsequently, "in a vision" (15. 1.); but he talks to him as he did to Adam and Noah—But the visible sign does not yet pass away. For, when the Lord made a covenant with Abraham, just after the manner of the ancient Hebrews, (15-9-10) though the terms of it were revealed to him in "deep sleep" (15-12-10&c) the actual ratification was made, as was the custom, by the Lord passing between the pieces of meat, as "a smoking furnace and a lamp of fire" (15. 17).

(iv) In Genesis 15.

Subsequently, however. the covenant is re-affirmed by God who "talked with" Abraham (17. 3.)

The Lord, next, comes "*down*" to Sodom and Gomorrah to "see whether they have done altogether
(V) In Genesis 18. according to the cry of it, which is come into him, "and if not," (he says) "I will know." (Genesis 18, 21).

Next we find the same. perceptive God-experience, distinctly, repeated in the case of Jacob:—

"And Jacob was left alone; and there wrestled a man with him until the breaking of the day. And when he saw he prevailed not against him (Jacob)—he said—Let me go, for the day breaketh. And he (Jacob) said, I will not let thee go, except thou bless me. And he (the wrestler) said unto him (Jacob) what is thy name? And he said, Jacob. And he said, thy name shall be called no
(VI) In Genesis 32. more Jacob, but Israel: for as a prince thou hast power with God, and with men, and hast prevailed. And Jacob asked him and said. Tell *me*, I pray thee, thy name. Wherefore *is* it *that* thou dost ask after my name? And he blessed him there. And Jacob called the name of the place PENIEL (ie the Face of God): for I have seen God *face to face*, and my life is preserved. (Genesis 32. 24-30 &c).

In Genesis 35, 9—15, is recorded another "appearance" of God to Jacob, and his converse with

him, and also how God pointed out the spot where Jacob had first talked to him, so that he might
(VII) In Genesis 35. build a pillar there, in memory of of the event;—"And God went up from him (Jacob) in the place where he talked with him. And Jacob set up a pillar in the place—and called the name of the place where God spake with him,—Bethel" (verses 10—15).

It would also be impossible to deny that the God-experience recorded of Moses in the Old Testament is also of a distinctly perceptive kind.

In Exod 3-2. where is recorded the first vision of Moses, we read—"the Angel of the Lord appeared unto him in a flame of fire out of the midst of a bush, and he looked, and behold ! the bush
VIII In Exodus 3. burned with fire, and the bush was not consumed. And Moses said, I will now turn aside, and see this great sight, why the bush is not burnt. And when the Lord saw that he turned aside to see, God called unto him out of the midst of the bush, and said, Moses, Moses. And he said, Here am I. etcs (verses 2-4)

A reference to Isaiah, 63, 9, tells us what the Angel of the Lord means,—it means not a mes-
(IX) In Israel 6. senger of the Lord, but his *presence* "In all their affliction he was afflicted, and the *angel* of *his presence* saved them etcs (Is. 63-9)

Subsequently, we read of the Lord going before the Israelites, in their journey through the wilderness,—"in a pillar of a cloud" by day and "in a pillar of fire" by night.(Ex. 13. 21.)

(X) In Exodns 13.

And all these bear ample, and it scems to us absolutely convincing evidence of the perceptive, the "sensible" or sensuous character of the earliest God-experience of the Hebrews.

(III) In Mahomedanism.

Even Maho mmed, the most iconoclastic, and in some sense, the most rationalistic of the founders of religion, though he did not *see* God, yet *heard* his voice in mount Horeb. If it be said it was not audition, but cognition, not a sensuous but a soul-experience, expressed in the terms of the sensuous only, still the actuality of the visions of his disciples—visions of him and Ali and others, could not be so explained away. Nor should we forget the comparatively advanced state of Arab consciousness and culture when Mahommed was born. Islam belongs, really, not to the perceptive but to the reflective state of religious evolution.

The perceptive element in Mahomedanism–in the visions of Mahommed and his disciples—though Islam, really, belongs to the reflective stage of religious evolution.

(IV) It cannot be entirely Subjective.

All these, however, disappear from the later Jewish records. It is no longer God himself who appears directly to man, but his angels,—bene-Elohim,—the sons of God as they are called, become messengers between God and man. Gradually even these pass out of the stage of Judaic religious thought and imagination, and not God, nor even his angels, but most frequently the "Voice of God," comes to the Prophets to communicate to them, and through them to the people of Israel, the wishes and admonitions of Yahveh, until we find in the New Testament that neither the visible presence of God, nor that of his angels, nor even his "voice" comes to man, but it is the Spirit of God that descends,—and here also in a visible form, though evidently symbolic—upon Jesus immediately after his baptism to declare that this is his Son in whom he is well-pleased. And the gradual dropping out, in these records, of the previous visions and auditions of God is extremely significant, as indicative of the fact that in the earliest stage, even according to Jewish tradition, man did hold intercourse with visible and audible

In later Jewish records, the angels came as messengers of God to man. In the next stage, we find the "voice of Gods" coming. At last, in the New Testament, the Spirit of God, in a visible form descends upon Jesus.

The early perceptive stage transcended so gradually can never be called entirely Subjective.

gods, and this vision, in any case, was not entirely subjective.

(V) Its end Sensuous.

The earliest phase of religion appears to have been either nature-worship, ancestor-worship or a combination of both. And, in every case, the object of man's earliest religion was cognisable, either directly or indirectly, by his senses. The nature-deities were all visible and audible objects, and the ancestors were also, in a way, such. They were human beings, having all the powers and functions and forms of visible men and women, though removed, by death, from the field of their earthly labours. These ancestors appeared, often times, to their children in dreams and thus testified to their existence, and not infrequently even indicated their wishes, their pleasure or their wrath, through the same psychological phenomena. And it is well-known that to the primitive man, his dream-life, though mystereous and awful, was not a bit less real than his waking-life, and that his dreams supplied much ampler materials for his crude but absolutely natural and

In nature-worship or ancestor-worship or a combination of both the object of worship is always cognisable by the senses.

E. G. the departed ancestors appearing in dreams.

unsophisticated religion, than even the experiences and activities of his waking hours. So, from whatever point of view we examine the earliest recorded or even the earlist conceivable, state of human religion, we find that it was almost entirely a product of man's sense-activities and his sense-life, the only life, that is, that he may be said to have had then. His deity was always something that he perceived by his senses. The end that he sought through his religion was the furtherance of his earthly, his animal, his sensuous life —he knew then of no other—the attainment of pleasure, and the avoidance of pain, both being almost entirely sensuous; and his mode of worship was also sensuous. Where religion appeared in the form of submission to custom or tradition alone, as we find it in some savage peoples, there also the motive was the safety and pleasure of the individual or of those who were dear and near to him.

In this stage the end of religion is also sensuous—attainment of pleasure and avoidance of pain.

(VI) It is unavoidable.

Nor, indeed, is there any warrant whatever, even in the experiences of the most developed forms of human religions, for looking down upon these primitive efforts of the human mind to reach itself out to the Absolute or Infinite, as belonging not only to a lower, but essentially and generically, an altogether different plane. For, can it be held that even Christianity or Islam, the two most iconoclastic religions of the world, has been able completely to get beyond every form of sensuousness in their religious ideals and cultures. What, for instance, are the deepest experiences of Islam? Do not these all gather around the relations that are realised by the faithful with the Prophet? And how are these cultivated? Is it not through the contemplation of the earthly life and even the fleshly form of the Hazrat, or of his immediate disciples, Ali or Abubekar and others? The lives of the Mahomedan saints all bear testimony to the fact that some, at least, of their profoundest spiritual experiences gathered around the vision of Mahommed and his personal friends and disciples. And every devout Mahomedan would, we think, unhesitatingly admit, that in the profoundest beatitudes known to Islam, the figure or the person of Mohammed is always or almost always present in the consciousness of the devotee. And the same remark applies to Christianity as

The deepest spiritual experiences of Islam and the Christian consciousness prove that though sensuousness indicates a lower stage of religious culture yet the most iconoclastic religions of the world can not always afford to get completely beyond every form of it. Thus it is not of a plane quite different from that of the higher religious experiences.

well. The profoundest experiences of the Christian consciousness have gathered around not only the character of Christ, in a vague or formless fashion, but around the figure of Jesus, especially of his figure on the cross. The *vision* of Christ on the cross is universally regarded as a very superior spiritual attainment in every form of Christian meditation, and St. Francis of Assisi, who so deeply realised this vision as to reproduce in his own body, the passion of Christ, has been almost universally accepted as the ideal Christian devotee. The figure of Christ, and that of the Madonna, are accepted institutions for spiritual discipline and culture in both the Catholic and the Greek Churches. They are not absolutely discarded by Protestantism either. They are found in the Anglican Church, for instance; and though some Protestant denominations have banished these figures from their Church, have they been able to put the vision of Christ on the cross altogether from their consciousness, or even from their religious exercises? On the contrary, do they not enthusiastically preach this vision as a vehicle of Christian worship and Christian culture? And those that have entirely banished it: have they gained or have they suffered in their religious and spiritual life by it?

(VII) It is Universal.

The fact really is that man's sense-perceptions forming an organic element of his life, constitute always an organic element also of his religion. Even the most modern of our religions, those that pretend to have known God as Spirit, and that try, therefore, to worship him, in spirit and in truth, have not, really, reached that super-sensuous state which they preach. Their God is found, at the final analysis, to be either a mere abstract idea, and if so, it is no doubt super-sensuous,—or a mere word, an empty sound,—an acoustic symbol, so to say, around which whatever religion they have sought to grow,—or it is some sensuous imagery, a poesy or a phantasy and nothing more. The meanings of sense-perceptions may and do vary as between a primitive and a civilised man, but the fact that these contribute the most vital elements to human religion seems to us to be Universal.

The perceptive or sensuous element is a Universal factor in human religion having a place even in the most modern of our religions. It appears in different forms in different stages.

(VIII) It is a Question of Fact not of Reality.

In any case we have it almost on the universal testimony of both ancient records and modern researches into the psychology of primitive life that in the earliest state of the evolution of religion, the object of human worship was always either visible objects or phenomena, or some visible social authority. Man does, in primitive culture, see and hear his God. This much is undeniable.

We are not, of-course, considering in this psychological study of our religious experiences, their objectivity or reality *i. e.* whether the true God appears, as He is, through them. We take them merely as facts through which the religious life of man progresses

And in studying the phenomena of religious evolution, we are not concerned here with the truth or falsehood of these visions and auditions,—truth that is, in the sense of their objective reality. It would be difficult to establish the objective reality of the experiences of even our more philosophical religions. But this question stands, however, outside the range of our investigation. We are considering here a mental or psychological phenomenon, namely the original ideas of man regarding the deity, and how they took their birth. The *truth* of the ideas, as a matter of actual experience, and the way in which they have grown up : this is what we are trying to understand ; and this truth is absolutely independent of the objectivity or reality of those ideas and ideals. A man may, for instance, jump off in a fright at the movement of a black creeper dangling before his face from the branch of a tree in a tropical jungle, taking it for a deadly viper, and the fact that what he got so frightened at was not a viper but a creeper, will not disprove the *truth* of his fears or the fact of his running away from it. Similarly the question here is not whether what primitive man saw and heard was in reality God as we have come to understand that concept, but whether his God-idea did or did not reveal itself through these visions and auditions ; and whether the feelings and activities that resulted from these visions and auditions were not what must be regarded as truly religious. And when we find that it was so, we can safely assert that the earliest known and conceivable phase of religious evolution is what may well be called naturalistic or perceptive.

And from such a point of view it is doubtless that the perceptive, forms the necessary earliest stage.

(IX) Forms and Characters of its Deities.

Nor is it altogether impossible to trace even the *form* and *character* of the deities or gods of this perceptive phase of human religions. The Vedic deities are indicated by their very names. Agni is fire, and no one who reads the texts of the Vedas dedicated to this god, can mistake his actual form or character. It is not possible, without doing great violence to the texts, to interpret the Vedic Agni in any but a purely natural sense. Agni, for instance, is described as having two,

The forms and characters of the Deities of the perciptive stage may be traced to their natural or social sources.

mothers, *dvimatrika*, which clearly refers to the production of fire, in that primitive age, by the help of the fire-drill, that is, by rubbing two pieces of sticks against each other. We are next told that it is a strange character of this God-Agni, that he eats up his parents immediateiy he is born. Like Agni, Varuna also is unmistakably this visible firmament, and so are Maruts,—the winds; and the heavenly twins,—the Aswini Kumars are without doubt the morning and evening twilight. Soma is the juice of the plant of that name which served as a beverage, possibly fermented and intoxicating, to the Vedic Aryans. Indra is sometimes the Sun, sometimes the clouds,—the holder of the thunderbolt, and sometimes, in later records, he seems to represent the entire hierarchy of the shining spheres overhead. Saraswati is distinctly a river, and we shall see while studying what Professor Max Muller calls the biography of these Vedic deities, how by an exceedingly natural and simple process, this Saraswati came to develop into the presiding Deity of all human arts and sciences, and even the inspirer of divine wisdom, and its personification. Vedic deities are of two classes, *devas and pitris*. The devas, as their name implies, represented nature forces and phenomena, especially those manifested in the heavens; the pitris—the fathers, represented the ancestors of

E.G. The Devas and the pitris of the Vedas convey to their worshippers forms and characters apprehended by the Senses.

the Vedic Aryans. And both these conveyed to their worshippers forms and characters easily appehended by the senses and what may be called the lower intellect of man. *

We have already referred to the oldest Hebrew records that have come down to us, where we find distinct traces of what we have called, the perceptive or naturalistic phase of primitive religion. It is difficult, however, to ascertain from these records, what was the actual *form* of these earliest perceptions of the Deity among the Semitic peoples. Both Elohim and Yahveh are, to us, mere names. We can find out from the Vedas what Agni, or Varuna, or the Maruts, and other Vedic deities meant in real, sensuous life. But what Elohim or Yahveh really meant similarly, is more than what we can say in the present state of our knowledge of Hebrew religion and Hebrew language. All that we know of Yahveh is that it was a mere sign among devout Hebrews, who expressed it by bringing together five characters of their Alphabet—Yodh, Alêph, Vow, Alêph and hê,—

It is difficult forus to ascertain now the actual forms of the earliest perceptions of the deity among the Semitic peoples.

Yahveh and Elohim are to us mere linguistic signs for God, But we do not know what actual natural or social experiences suggested those unpronouncable combinations of letters.

* For illustrations (1) Egyptian, (2) Babylonian and Assyrian. Mytholgy; Vide-Hibbert Lectures; and (3) Primitive culture—Vide Tylor and Spencer.

without any *nookta* or vowel sounds being joined to them, and the combination, therefore, stood as a mystery which could not even be pronounced. A similar mysterious combination also appears in in the Scriptures of Islam, namely, *aleph, lain and meem,* but without any vowel sounds and which also is, consequently, an unpronouncable word. But *aleph and lain,* in the form of *El,* is a term common to both Arabic and Hebrew and seems to be the oldest word for God in the Semitic languages. We find it in the Arabic Allah, as well as in the Hebrew Elohim. This is all, that we know of Elohim also. But what was the original meaning of El or Elohim,—what of Yahveh? Do these terms refer to something that the primitive Hebrew or Arab, or the common ancestors of both saw or heard or felt in his nature-environment, or were they suggested by his experiences of or relations with social authority to which he was subject? These are vital questions. El-Elohim is rendered into English by God Almighty. Here is evidently the idea of might, strength, power. But whence derived? What was it that suggested this term to the early Semitic man, as a word for invincible might or power? Did the perception of might that gave Elohim as a name for the godhead, originally grow through man's contact with some nature-force, or with his social

El- Elohim rendered into English by "God Almihgty" suggests the idea of might or power perceived in nature or society.

authority. These are pertinent questions here, and a satisfactory answer to these questions can alone *reveal* the actual object, the *original* experience which evoked this god-sense in the primitive peoples from whose records the present Old Testament books were clearly compiled.

But if Elohim suggests its origin in the perception of power or might, whether in Nature or Society we cannot say, Yahveh seemes to our mind to suggest its origin somewhat more definitely in social experience alone. For Yahveh is, undoubtedly, the real God of the covenant in the Hebrew Scriptures, though what was the original form through which the percept first commenced to grow is more than what we can say for is ever likely to discover from existing records. But Elohim, clearly, belonged to an earlier period of the evolution of Judaic religion than Yahveh. In the Old Testament, though Yahveh refers to his Covenant with Abraham he presents himself in this new name for the first time to Moses. It is not unlikely, therefore, that Yahveh came in at a later and more developed stage, when Judaism was passing gradually out of the early perceptive and naturalistic phases, and consequently when the old vision of God had commenced to grow dim and the process of generalisation and abstraction had

Yahveh, the real God of the covenant, came in, perhaps, at a more developed stage of Judaism when perception was giving its place to generalisation and abstraction.

already started in Hebrew thought to a more or less extent.

(B) The Reflection Stage.

But though religion takes its birth, naturally, in the sense-life and the sense-experiences of man, it soon commences to transcend these. For, our senses themselves gradually reveal their own inadequacy even to explain their own workings. They cannot permanently confiine the thoughts, the ideas, the emotions and the activities of man, with the narrow limits of what may be called a mere perceptive life. With the expansion of experience, primitive man, like the child In civilisation which necessarily reproduces in itself every phase and process of both the physiological and the pychological evolution of the race,—commences gradually to compare one thing with another, and thereby to think, to reason, to reflect, and thus slowly but surely to transcend the apparent evidence and suggestion of the senses, and rise, step by step, to a consciousness of the super-sensuous. We see this process of slow evolution very clearly in the development of early Vedic religion, where almost all the gods, Agni, Varuna, Rudra, Indra, 'Sara-

(1) But the limits of the senses are soon overtaken by the power of comparison and reflection.

swati, that clearly took their birth in the sense-experience of the primitive Indo-Aryans, are gradually vested with super-sensuous and ethical properties. Agni which took its birth from the fire-drill comes to be conceived as existing, in a latent form—in the shape, as it is subsequently put, of an unmanifested cause—in the two pieces of wood constituting the drill, and though *unseen* its substance or form is, thus, never destroyed, and this all-pervasiveness is transferred to inner experiences of man ; and Agni, finally, becomes even an all-knowing God. Similerly Varuna too, first apprehended as this visible firmament covering and overlooking every living and moving, as well as every inanimate and fixed thing, comes gradually to be vested with the idea of over-lordship and omnipresence and slowly, with that of omniscience also, until the Vedic worshipper is able to cry out, almost like the Hebrew psalmist, that Varuna knows his uprising and down-sitting, and can find him out from the most secret place of the earth. In studying the biography of these Vedic gods, we shall see how gradually these super-sensuous concepts gathered, by a very easy and natural psychological process, around the original sensuous and sensible ideas of the god-head of the early Vedic texts until in the Upanishads we find a phase of religion that

E. G. attribution of unseen substantiality, causality and all-pervasiveness to Agni and overlordship, omnipresence and even intelligence to Varuna.

has grown absolutely beyond all tinge or suspicion of sensuousness. But even these books themselves,

Supersensuousness most manifest in the Upanishads. But the transition from the sensuous still visible there.

with all their super-sensuous and subjective emphasis do bear occasional testimony to the original sensuousness of Vedic religion and to their growth out of it. *The Kenopanishad* of the *Sama Veda*, distinctly states how its questionings about the super-sensuous, arose out of its contemplation and examination of sensuous experience. It starts with the question :—

केनेषितं पतति प्रेषितं मनः
केन प्राणः प्रथमः प्रैति युक्तः ।
केनेषितां वाचमिमां वदन्ति
चक्षुः श्रोत्रं क उ देवो युनक्ति ?

"By whom directed, does the mind move to its own objects? Under whose guidance, does the vital power, the first of the internal organs, perform its functions? Under whose leading are these words uttered! Who is that God who leads the eyes and the ears to their own objects ?"

And it shows that the Vedic Hindu had, already, commenced long before the time this Upanishad was taught, to reflect upon and analyse his sense-experiences, and had found out the utter

ii. This reflective stage began before the time of the Upanishads, and gradually established the inadequacy of sensuous objects as objects of worship.

inadequacy of the senses to explain and interpret themselves. And when the insufficiency of the senses themselves was thus realised by him, it could not, possibly, take long, after this, for the Vedic Hindu to discover the inability of the old naturalistic and perceptive deities to justify their place and character as objects of human worship, and we, therefore, find them dismissed almost with scant courtesy, by the devotees of the Upanishads.

न तत्र सूर्यों भाति न चन्द्र तारकं
नेमा विद्युतो भान्ति कुतोऽयमग्निः ।
तमेव भान्तमनुभाति सर्व्वं
तस्य भासा सर्व्वमिद विभाति ॥

There (in Brahman) the sun does not shine, neither the moon, nor the stars, nor do these lightnings shine there: how then shall this fire (illumine it)? All these shine after Him, the Shining (One). By his light are all these illumined.

* Kathopanishad. Chap. II. Valli II. 15th verse.

(I) The Emotional and Volitional Phases of Religion.

(i) The emotional and the volitional phases of religion determined by the intellectual phase.

Religion always concerns the whole life of man; and it has, therefore, three departments, so to say, corresponding to the three aspects of the human life, namely, those of (1) intellection, (2) emotion, and (3) volition. The first concerns man's ideas regarding his deity, the second concerns his feelings towards his deity, and third his activities in relation to his deity. And the character of the second and third aspect of man's religion is always determined by the first. His emotions towards his God are the direct fruits of his knowledge of, or his ideas concerning that God, and his religious activities or acts of worship are always determined by these emotions. In the earliest, or what we have called, the perceptive phase of human religion, as the Deity is an object of man's senses, so his religious emotions are also, really, sensations, and have reference more to his physical than to his inner life, as we understand that life to be. Fear is the most dominant feeling in all primitive religion, fear arising out of the apprehension of some physical pain or loss. And from the records of very primitive peoples, like the cannibals of the Pacific or of Central Africa,

(ii) In the earliest stage of religion the ideas of God received through the senses arouse the emotion of fear, and the devotional activities consist in magic, sorcery &c.

it seems that the deities in this phase of early religion, are almost always regarded as malevolent, and consequently magic, incantation, sorcery, —these constitute the chief elements of worship here, if worship at all it may be called; and sorcerers and medicine-men are their priests. Possession is a very common religious experience in this stage, and magic, sorcery, and the other concomitants of cannibal religion, seem to grow out of these curious nervous and psychological phenomena. The object of worship here is not propitiation, really, but subjugation or expulsion of the deity which clearly is engaged in doing evil to the children of man. And the most common forms of these magics, incantations, and exorcisms, are the infliction of distinctly visible torments on the subject. Consequently, even primitive magic does not work through absolutely unseen agencies. In the later phases, hypnotism and other allied psychological phenomena came to be closely associated with magic and sorcery; and the agencies became consequently more or less unseen and mysterious; but in the earliest stages, these were clearly visible, and worked through purely physical or physiological means.

We do not find this phase, however, very markedly, if we find it at all, in the Vedic records. There is, no doubt, a good deal of exorcism, and magic, and incantations, in the Vedas. Indeed, the best part, perhaps of the *Atharva Veda* may be said to consist of these. They are, possibly, the contribution of the non-Aryan and aboriginal tribes of India, to the Vedic culture and religion, which first opposed and subsequently, with the wonderful adaptibility of all ethnic systems, quietely absorbed these aboriginal ideas and ideals into themselves. But whatever their origin, these exorcisms and incantations generally refer, not to the real Vedic gods, but to the evil spirits, the Asuras and the Rakshases, as well as to one's enemies-the unknown and known causes of the ills that befall man. Even if magic, sorcery, incantations, and exorcists and medicine-men, be accepted as representing the earliest forms of human religion, we find but scant records and recollections of those in the scriptures and traditions of the great world-religions. The records of the past history and evolution of which seem to refer, clearly, to a later and higher phase of these religions; and though fear is still found to be the dominant motive of religious works and worship, the method adopted is propitiation, and no longer subjugation or ex-

Illustration from the Vedas.

(i) They refer to evil spirits and enemies of men and hence not to Vedic gods proper.

(ii) The great world-religions have very scanty record of this stage, and in them even fear leads to propitiation, but not subjugation or expulsion of the deity.

pulsion of the deity by the infliction of counter-punishment or counter-injury on it.

The propitiation of fire by *hom*, and subsequently when other gods were conceived, to make fire the bearer of oblations to gods speak of a higher culture of the Indo-Aryans.

And the form in which the god or gods are sought to be propitiated corresponds, very naturally, to their sensuous or sensible character, in the earlier phases of religious evolutions. In Vedic ritualism, *hom* or offering of clarified butter and sacred and scented herbs to fire, constitutes, possibly, the earliest form, and it was a distinct and visible mode of feeding the fire, and Fire was, as we are told, the first-born of the gods, in the Vedas. When the other gods came to appear upon the Vedic altar, the Vedic devotee must have been perplexed somewhat as to the means of making offerings to them. Varuna could not, possibly, be so directly worshipped as Fire. Neither could the Maruts, nor the Aswini Kumars, nor Rudra; indeed, none others of the Vedic gods could be so directly tended and so visibly worshipped as Fire. How to make offerings to them, must have, therefore, been a perplexing problem to the simple-minded Vedic Hindu; and with characteristic aptitude he seemed, subsequently, to have solved it, by setting up Agni or Fire as the messenger of the gods,—he who, not only accepted these himself, but also carried the offerings of the children of man to their heavenly lords and gods. Here is suspicion of a somewhat advanced state of culture, no doubt; but we cannot say exactly when these other gods also were born in the consciousness of the primitive Indo-Aryans. One thing, however, is clear, and it is this, namely, that Agni as jungle-fire must have received the attention of his worshippers much earlier than any of the heavenly gods. Agni was, in this particular form, distinctly a terrestrial phenomenon; and terrestrial phenomena received necessarily much earlier attention from primitive man than the celestial phenomena, specially those associated with light and darkness. Even the Upanishads, belonging admittedly to a much later and higher phase of ancient Indo-Aryan evolution, record the perceptive character of the ancient worship of Fire by the Vedic devotees, though condemning it as incapable of producing any lasting spiritual good.*

The terrible jungle fire attracted earliest attention.

(iii) But even the Upanishads refer to fire worship though as incapable of producing lasting Benefit.

यदा लेलायते ह्यर्चिः समिद्धे हव्यवाहने ।
तदाज्यभागावन्तरेणाहुतीः प्रतिपादयेच्छ्रद्धयाहुतम् ॥

*(18) Agni is not only called the priest of the gods and their messenger,—but also (1) Bharata, *i.e.* the *bearer* of the oblations to the gods, (2) Rathi the carrier of sacrifices to the gods, (3) As-patram—the mouth-vessel, the offering spoon of the gods. (4) The cup from which the gods drink.—See Sathapatha-Brahmana, I Khanda, 4 Adh. 2 Brahmana.

(19) Agni is also described as the Leader—*Agrani*—the commander of the divine forces, who led the gods in their wars against

काली कराली च मनोजवा च
सुलोहिता या च सुधूम्रवर्णा ।
स्फुलिङ्गिनी विश्वरुची च देवी
लेलायमाना इति सप्त जिह्वाः ॥
एतेषु यश्चरते भ्राजमानेषु
यथाकालं चाहुतयो ह्याददायन् ॥ *

"When, on the fire being kindled, the flame moves about, the worshipper should pour libation with reverence, etc. Kali, Karali, Manojava, Sulohita, Sudhumravarna, Sphulingini, and the bright Bishvaruchi, these are the seven moving tongues (of the sacrificial fire). When one performs sacrifices at the time those flames are kindled, offering libations in proper time,—attains to the region of the Supreme God."

II. Ritualistic and external method of worship in the Perceptive Stage.

In the earliest phase of religious evolution, so far as we can discover it either in ancient records

the Asuras and Rakshases. This function was subsequently ascribed to Indra, and the old idea of Agni as the general of the gods may have considerably helped, subsequently, the syntheses of Agni, Indra, Surya etc. into "the One True"—*Ekam Sat*—found in the well-known Sukta of the Tenth Mandala of the Rig Veda.

Ekamsadbipra Vahudha Vadanti etc.

* Mundakopanishad. I (ii) 2, 4, and 5.

or in the life and institutions of primitive races still existing, as the god-idea is universally what we have characterised as perceptive, or what Max Mullar calls naturalistic or what is described by Old Testament scholars as particularistic,—so the method of worship is also universally ritualistic and external. But the character of this externality is, however, not the same everywhere, because the nature of the original religious emotions or relations is not the same among all races. In considering the earliest phases of religious worship as found, for instance, in the Vedas and the Old Testament, we observe a very wide difference in the character. In the Vedic religion and ritualism we find what may be called a most pronounced note of fellowship between the devotees and their deities. There is a distinct note of friendship, mixed with that of awe and fear, of course, in Vedic chants and *mantras*, which we miss very much in the earliest phase of Judaic religion. The relations between Agni or Indra or the other Vedic deities and their worshippers, are touched always with love and affection, and these gods are very often, if not uniformly, addressed and approached in the terms of the family and social relations. But it is very different in the case of Yahveh and his people. There we find the rela-

(a) The character of externality different in different religions.

(i) The note of fellowship between the devotees and their deities in the Vedic religion

tion to be almost rigidly legalistic and commercial.

(ii) The rigidly legalistic and commercial relation in the Yahveistic religion.

Indeed, it must necessarily have been, owing to the contractual or covenantal character of the Yahveistic religion itself. Yahveh enters into a covenant with the ancestors of the Israelite people, by which he agrees to be their God and Lord, and give to them and to their seed, the inheritance of the earth, and they, on their part, agree to serve him to the absolute exclusion of other gods, and follow his laws and his injunctions.

Motive for its observance—reward and punishment.

There is little or no room for the play of any real affection or love in such a purely legal and commercial transaction; and we find no trace of these softer human sentiments in the religion of Israel until we come to the times of Jeremiah. Indeed, the word love as expressing a religious sentiment first occurs in the Book of Deuteronomy.*

It is a contract made collectively and not individually, and hence no room for human emotions.

In all the previous records the motives for the observance of the Yahveistic law is presented as mere earthly rewards, as its violation is threatened to be met likewise with earthly punishments. The whole scheme is external. In fact, the covenant or

* Vide the Book of Deuteronomy. Ch. 6. 5. "And thou shalt love the Lord thy God with all thine heart, and with all thy soul, and with all thy might." Again, 30. 6. This last verse is significant as showing how the earlier perceptive, and external, and

contract between Yahveh and the people of Israel having been made collectively with the whole race, and not with individual members of it, there was little room for the play of any human emotions, as there was absolutely no sense of individual responsibility also, in the earlier religion of the Hebrews. It took a long time indeed, for any kind of real inwardness even of an ethical type, to grow in Judaism and a distinct ethical note we find for the first time, in the Prophets Amos and Hosea.* In the pre-prophetic period, Judaism seems, thus to have been, in its own way as much external, objective, and perceptive, in spite of its somewhat supersensuous ideas of the Godhead, both in its forms of worship and in its general religious life as the ritualism of the Vedas.

Its inwardness of the ethical type took a very long time to grow on account of this externality.

In fact, animal sacrifices are common to both the early Hindu and the early Hebrew religion. Attempts have been made to impart a superior

(b) Animal Sacrifice came to the early stage of both religions.

covenantal ideal of religions had already commenced to be transferred, and become reflective, internal, and ethical. Here, in 30-6, we read of a new signification of circumcision—"the Lord thy God will circumcise thine heart, and the heart of thy seed, to love the Lord thy God with all thine heart, and with all thy soul, that thou mayest live."

* Vide the Book of Amos and Hosea.

ethical significance to the sacrificial religion of Israel, and to interpret these as a cruder symbol of the great ethical and spiritual truth revealed through the passion of Christ,—the greatest sacrifice ever made on earth —that of the "only Begotten Son of God,"—for the salvation of the world. But there is nothing absolutely in the idea of sacrifice as found in Judaism, specially in its earlier perceptive or particularistic state, to justify the reading of any ethical significance into it. The only thing common to both the Judaic and the Christian idea of sacrifice is its legality, and absolutely, nothing else. The sacrifice of Christ propitiates the offended majesty of outraged Divine Law, and the sin-offerings and peace-offerings of the Jews had the same idea in them. Beyond this pure legalistic idea there is nothing really common between the Jewish conception of sacrifice as found in the earlier books, and the Christian conception, in which a new element that of Infinite love and tenderness, entered to raise it from the discharge of a contractual and legalistic obligation, to the spontaneous outpouring of Eternal Love and Infinite Sympathy. Indeed, both the Vedic and the Talmudic

(i) Attempts to interpret ethically the early sacrifices of the Hebrews as cruder symbols of the great Sacrifice of Christ.

The interpretation far-fetched.

The only common feature is legalism.

(ii) The new element of infinite love and tenderness in Christianity.

conception of sacrifice have in them the common idea of propitiating the deity by making acceptable offerings to it. Both are external acts, and have no inner significance in them. The difference between the two being this, namely, that while the Vedic sacrifices were made in the spirit, more or less, of friendly offerings, in the expectation, though, of favours to come, and were, thus, partly of a spontaneous character, the Talmudic sacrifices were made distinctly in the discharge of a clear contractual obligation, in the spirit of rigid legalism, and were not, therefore, allied to any necessary sentiment of love or affection or gratitude. These sentiments did grow, no doubt, in Judaism in its later developments, and they abound in the Psalms, and also are found in some of the Prophets, but that was long after Judaism had passed beyond the primitive period we are here considering, when, indeed, even the old contractual conception of religious duty, as well as that of the God of Israel as a mere party to a rigid civil contract or covenant, had been largely modified partly as the result of the inner evolution of Judaic life and thought, and partly as that of foreign contact and influence.

(iii) Propitating the Deity by external acts is the common idea of sacrifice in both the Vedic and the Talmudic religion.

(iv) The sentiments of love and gratitude found in the Vedic idea of sacrifice, developed very late in Judaism through inner evolution and foreign contact.

(III) Transition to the Reflective Stage.

And, as we have already said, such transformations were bound to result from the expansion of human experience and the growth of reflection. And the course of religious evolution may, therefore, be said to proceed, from the earliest or perceptive phase to the reflective phase. If, thus, the earliest phase be called Perceptive, the subsequent phases, for a long time, may well be characterised as merely Reflective; because these phases distinctly grow out of man's thoughts and reflections on his primitive sense life and sense experiences. And as we have named the first or earliest known or conceivable phase of religious evolution, Perceptive, in preference to Prof. Caird's Objective, to avoid the possible suspicion of the presence and operation of any sort of reflection or reasoned process in early religious growth, so we prefer to call the subsequent phases of religious evolution Reflective in preference to Prof. Caird's Subjective, because, as we have already shown, though we do not find a truly subjective phase in all religions, we do find these reflective phases not only in the records of all the great world-religions, but in their earlier

(i) It consists in the reflections on early religious experiences.

(ii) This phase common in all world-religions should better be called Reflective than Subjective, for it refers to thought as distinct from sense perception, and not properly to Metaphysical Speculation.

forms, we find them even in the history of primitive culture. The term Subjective indicates the birth of real philosophical or metaphysical speculations, but reflective raises no such anticiptions. We find evidence of these speculations in the Upanishads, which may, indeed, claim to be the only speculative books accepted as Scriptural authority in the entire range of the religious literature of mankind. But there are parts even of the Rig Veda, characterised by Max Muller as the oldest existing records of the great Aryan family, that distinctly show that the Vedic Hindu had already commenced to think, to reason, to reflect, upon the primitive religious ideas and practices of his race long before the birth of the Upanishads. And we find the same process of reflection—though nothing that might be classified with the philosophical speculation of the Upanishads—in the Old Testament records, as well as in the records of ancient Egypt and Chaldœa. Indeed, we can hardly characterise even the most advanced teachings of the Prophets of Israel, which represent surely a very developed state of Judaic culture and religion, as really speculative, in the sense in which we apply this term to the Upanishads. In the evolution of Judaism, there was, no doubt, a speculative, though not a truly subjective phase. Perhaps we

(a) The Upanishads and even parts of the Rig Veda are the records of the earliest human religious Speculations.

(b) Reflection in the Old Testament and in the ancient records of Egypt and Chaldœa.

(c) Reflective Judaism has nothing like the subjectivism of the Upanishads.

find evidences of these speculations in what are called the Maccabbean Psalms, aud in a more marked degree in the Cabillistic interpretations of the Jewish Law and the Prophets. But these are, practically absent from the Old Testament records, represent in its higher phases, simply what may be called reflective Judaism, as it indicates, in its primitive forms, the perceptive phases of Hebrew evolution. Buddhism, Christianity, and Islam, representing the credal phase of Hinduism, Judaism, and the ancient religion of the Arab people, respectively, came into being in the reflective state of these older religions, and all these, in their way, did, naturally, develop various speculative systems, representing higher and more complex phases of religious evolution. But both Christianity and Islam can hardly claim to have been at all speculative at their birth. Speculative Christianity took its birth really through Greek influence, in the interpretations put upon the life, death, and teachings of Jesus, by St Paul and the author of the Johanine Gospel, and specially by the Alexandrian Fathers, Origen, Clement, Tertullion and others; while we find the

(d) Buddhism, Christianity and Islam representing the credal phase of Hinduism, Judaism and and ancient religion of the Arabs respectively originated in the reflective stage of those older religions and naturally developed many Speculative Systems.

(e) Both Christianity and Islam were first simply reflective and became specelative only long afterwords.

growth of a speculative theology out of the teachings of the Prophet and the Koran, most distinctly in the writings of the Matazalas and the Suphis. But both Christianity and Islam, in their original forms, do not represent a speculative, but simply a reflective phase of religious evolution.

(iii) Subjectivity indicates a state of antithesis but Reflection covers both antithesis and synthesis.

While the word subjective indicates, really, an antithetical state of religious evolution, this term Reflective covers both this and the synthetical states of it, and is, applicable, therefore, to a much longer course of evolution than Prof. Caird's Subjective. And, as a matter of actual history, every religion has been passing almost continually, through repeated processes of thesis, antithesis and synthesis in the course of its growth. It is present even in what we have characterised as the Perceptive or Naturalistic state, as it is in the later Reflective state. What differentiates this state, from the earlier perceptive state is not its subjectivity, but its super-sensuousness.

(iv) Essence of reflection is not Subjectivity, but Super-sensuousness—a sense of the Unseen.

A growing sense of the Unseen is the principal characteristic of this phase of religious evolution, though the actual conception of this Unseen varies very widely in different religions. In some religions, as in that of the Upanishads, the Unseen is apprehended as the Absolute, as it is understood in the

(a) In the Upanishads the Unssen is Infinite and Absolute.

highest philosophical or metaphysical speculations,—as the Universal and the Infinite. In others, as in Judaism, the Unseen is represented

(b) In Judaism a Non-natural and Magnified man

practically, as, what Mathew Arnold called, a Non-Natural and Magnified Man. The Upanishads, however, do not represent the earliest phase of what may be called Reflective Hinduism. That phase is found in the Vedas themselves, and more markedly, as we shall see when studying Vedic Hinduism, in the exegetes and

(c) Hinduism Reflective simply in the Vedas and in the exegetes and apologetics of Vedic naturalism but Speculative in the Upanisads which came long afterwards.

apologetics of Vedic Naturalism, which sought to harmonise the primitive, perceptive religion of the Vedas with the earliest doubts and questionings of the Hindu mind. These doubts and questionings really represent the first movement of reflection in Vedic religion. The Upanishads came long after these; and there are traces of an anthropomorphic phase, even in Hinduism, prior to the speculative phase, seen in the Upanishads or the Vedantas.

(C) The Imaginative or Idealistic Stage.

In the growth of these anthropomorphic conceptions concerning the godhead, imagination, naturally, plays a very important part. And the evolution of religion commences, thus, to branch out into two lines in this Reflective state, one of which develops religious speculation, creates theologies, seeks to discover a rational ground and justification for religious beliefs and practices, and the other develops religious poetry, cultivates the religious imagination, and creates those profound mysteries of the spiritual life that subsequently become the very soul and essence of every higher religion.

(I) Play of imagination in religious evolution creating anthropo morphism and religious poetry.

Reflection proper creates theology and discovers rational ground of religion.

(II) The essence of higher religion in the pro found mysteries created by imagination.

'As imagination bodies forth,
The forms of things unknown, the poet's pen
Turns them into shapes, and gives to airy
nothing.
A local habitation anda name'.

So does the fancy or frenzy or the imagination of the devotee in religious history everywhere. This process is never absent, indeed, from religious history at any stage, or phase of it. But in the earliest or perceptive or naturalistic state, sense and sentiment work simultaneously, and religious perceptions and religious imagination exist together in an undifferentiated form. This is natural and necessary in the state of homogeneity, the earliest stage or phase of every evolutionary process. In the later state, what we have characterised as the Reflective state,—which is essentially a state of differentiation, though repeatedly followed by higher and higher integrations, the old homogeneity between sense and sentiment is more or less disturbed. Reflection takes up, so to say, the sense-perceptions, and puts off the immediate play of sentiment around them, at least for a time. And sentiment thus put off are really sentiments killed, and it is the function of Imagination always to revive and resuscitate delayed or dead sentiments. Religious Imagination, thus, properly, so-called, takes its birth only in the Reflective and not in the unreflective, naturalistic or perceptive phases of religious evolution.

(III) Imagination undifferentiated in the perceptive stage and put off through early reflection reasserts itself in later reflection.

Thus, we find in actual religious history that after the earliest or perceptive state or phases of religious evolution, there are, everywhere,—what may well be called these Reflective phases, and following these, there are the Imaginative phases, the highest, indeed, that have so far been evolved in the religious his-

(IV) Thus the imaginative phases coming, in a sense, after the reflective represent the highest stage discovered upto date.

tory of the human race. Whether in Hinduism, or Buddhism, or Christianity or Islam, these Imaginative phases stand still as the high-water mark of religious culture or spiritual life. What Prof Caird calls the Universal stage of religious evolution, is really, characterised by a very high note of idealism. In the earliest stage, according even to Prof. Caird, god-idea is objective, that is particularistic. In his second or subjective stage, god-idea is subjective ; that is here, evidently, the consciousness of the Deity or the ultimate reality takes the form of what is called the Abstract Universal. And, in his third and last or Universal stage, it takes the shape of what is called the Concrete Universal. But though Philosophy establishes the truth of the Concrete Universal in its own way, following its own methods of study and research, Religion, when it seeks to realise it, as an actual spiritual experience, has, of necessity, to accept the guidance of what is called Religious Imagination. All idealisation demands an exercise of the Imagination ; and the supreme idealisation which reveals matter, so to say, as the thought of God concretised, and man as the Spirit

(V) The Stage which Prof Caird calls Universal is philosophically characterised by the idea of the Concrete Universal established through the dialectic method but is actualised through spiritual experiences possible only under the guidance of higher imagination which leads to an idealism realising the Spirituality of matter and the Divinity of man.

of God incarnated, can only be possible through the exercise of the most superior kind of this faculty.

Indeed, though some people, in our age, may try to deduce some kind of a religion out of their own special philosophy of life, historically, that is, in the general experience of mankind, religions have not grown out of philosophies but philosophies have, almost always, grown out of religion. In other words, as in the development of every science, actual experience has preceded the investigation and discovery of general laws and principles, so also here, the actual religious experiences of man have universally preceded the development of his religious philosophy or theology. These latter have grown, almost everywhere, out of man's attempt to discover a rational basis and justification of his actual religious or spiritual experiences.

(VI) Religious imaginations leading to higher religious experiences precede philosophy of religion and make it possible by supplying materials.

Thus, Hindu philosophy has grown out of the inner mental and spiritual experiences of the Hindu ; Buddhist philosophy, similarly, out of the ethical and spiritual experience of the Buddhist ; Christian and Islamic philosophies, similarly, have grown out of the actual moral and emotional experience, of the Christian and the Moslem saints and devotees. Religious imagination takes precedence, therefore, of philosophical or meta-

History of the world-religions establishes the truth of the statement.

physical speculations in the history of religious evolution everywhere.

Nor can we summarily dismiss these imaginative experiences as mere figments of the fancy. Language in drawing a distinction between fancy and imagination has corroborated the evidence of human experience, regarding the truth and reliability of the latter. Indeed, most, if not all, of our positive scientific truths, principles, or laws are the products, absolutely, of the Imaginative Faculty. All our generalisations are, really, the children of the Imagination. Scientific laws are not apprehended by the senses, nor are they capable of any "sensible" or sensuous verification. The senses apprehend only particulars of our experience, it is the function of the imaginative faculty to peer beyond these particulars and discover the general or universal truths or principles underlying them. Scientific Imagination discovers the highest truths of science. Similarly Religious Imagination reveals the profoundest truths of the spiritual life. The one is as much a witness unto truth as the other.

(VII) Religious imagination is not fancy but the faculty which corresponds to scientific imagination, the fruitful source of all general principles of science.

(VIII) It discovers the religious ideas and ideals, only the particular applications of which can be the matters of our religious experience.

The Imaginative Faculty exercises, thus, the highest function in our mental and spiritual life. Its function is everywhere, whether in science

(IX) In art, science and religion, imagination thus carries us from the actual to the ideal.

or in art or in religion,—to transcend the limitations of the real and carry the reason, the emotions, and the spirit of man on its heavenly wings, on to the realms of the Ideal.

(X) The Idealistic stage, then, is the highest stage of Religious Evolution.

And, idealisation is an essential feature of the third, or the highest stage of religious evolution, as discussed by Prof. Caird. His Universal stage is essentially, the Idealistic stage. The highest or the universal stage of Christian evolution is that wherein Christ stands universalised in humanity, and thus the love and service of humanity become identified with the love and service of God or Christ. But how is this to be realised in actual inner experience, except through the help of the imaginative faculty? The Philosophy of the Absolute may have revealed to Prof. Caird and others of his School, the rational ground and justification of the Universal Christianity; but a Universal Christ-consciousness had been realised by Christian Saints and devotees, through the exercise of their Religious Imagination, long before Hegel sought to discover its philosophical or rational meaning and significance.

(a) In Christianity it was realised in Christ universalised in humanity thus identifying the love and service of God or Christ with love and service of humanity.

(b) The idea was realised in the imagination of the Christian saints and devotees long before it found its expression and justification in the Hegelian philosophy.

In tracing the historical growth of the religious phenomena, therefore, we may very safely state that in the earliest phase, religion is everywhere perceptive and sensuous, gradually, however, it becomes reflective and supersensuous, and finally it becomes, essentially, idealistic or imaginative. And if we have to divide, for the convenience of the students of the religious experiences of man, the history or course of religious evolution into definite phases or stages at all, we must call the first phase Perceptive, the second Reflective, and the third Imaginative, from the fact that though perception, reflection and imagination are all present at every state or stage of the religious phenomena, in the earliest states perception dominates reflection and imagination both; subsequently reflection dominates both perception and imagination, and ultimately imagination or idealisation dominates both perception and reflection. This, it seemes to us, is, in most general terms, the history of Religious Evolution. The Evolution of particular religions must, therefore, be studied in the light of this general or universal process or principle or law.

Conclusion:—Hence the Perceptive, the Reflective and the Imaginative are three principal Stages in the Evolution of Religion though in each earlier Stage the later stage or stages exist in a suppressed form.

History of the Evolution of any religion should be studied in the light of these stages of growth.

§ 3. Evolution does not Explain Original Differences among Religions.

But this general or universal process or principle or law of religious evolution, will not be able to explain and interpret all the endless varieties and complexities of the religious phenomena. By following it, we may be able to arrange and classify the mixed up records of the ancient world-religions, and by the application of this loicgal test, we may, thus, fix an approximate chronological succession among these records, and build up a more or less connected and intelligible story of that past evolution of these religions. But it will not help us to trace the causes of the wide divergences that exist, both in the character and history between these world-religions. We have already indicated one of the causes of this divergence, namely the difference in the emphasis that different religions have laid from almost pre-historic times, on the one or the other of the two aspects of the *Not—Me*, out of man's contact and conflict with which his reliigon seems to have grown everywhere. But this difference in the emphasis on either the Natural or the Social aspect of the Not-Me, of the different

(i) The process indicated above helps us to arrange and classify the facts of different world-religions for a consistent study

(ii) It will not help us to trace the Causes of difference between them which is mainly due to the difference of emphasis on the natural or the social aspect of the Not-me.

religions, does not explain their divergences fully. And a philosophy or science of Religion that fails to do so, cannot fully justify its claims as an interpreter of the religious phenomena in general. In any case it cannot pretend to have discovered the laws or principles of religious evolution.

(iii) It is the function of the philosophy or Science of religion to explain their differences in interpreting religious experiences of men.

For, all evolution is change in permanence. Every form of change or differentiation does not belong to the evolusionary process; but only such as preserve the continuity of the original class or kind or species, which is always discoverable under every change of form or even of functions, and where not apparent, this continuity may still be traced historically. Biological evolution, thus, always works upon two essential factors, namely, heredity and environment, the one representing the element of permanence and the other explaining the causes of change or variation, resulting from the operation of the law of natural selection. In working out the law of evolution in the growth of the religious phenomena, therefore, we have, first of all, to discover the element of permanence in religion in general. In defining religion as the attempt of

(iv) Evolution is change in Permanence thus always preserving a Continuity.

(v) Of its two essential factors, heredity represents the element of permanence and environment that of change.

man to adjust himself to his Not-me, we have already indicated this element. Both man and his Not-me, in its dual aspect of nature and society, constitute thus, the permanent factor in all religious evolution; and changes in the religious experiences of man, may be well traced, generally, to his changed notion of himself or his altered estimates of his Not-Me. It is these changes that, really, account for the evolution of religion from the Perceptive to the Reflective and from the Reflective to the Imaginative states or phases of its growth. But this is the general scheme of religious evolution, and though these phases are observed in all religions, at one point or other of their history, the differences that are noticed between one religion and another are not adequately, if they are at all, explained by a reference to these different phases of religious evolution. For these differences are not merely those of stages, like those observed, for instance, between a tadpole and a frog, or between a baby, a boy, and a young and an old man. They are observed in religions that distinctly occuppy the same plane of historic evolution. Judaism, for instance, even in its earliest or perceptive stage appears as essentially differ-

Man and his Not-me constitute the permanent element in religious evolution and changes in religious experience through changed ideas of himself and his surroundings represent the element of change.

(vi) Principles of evolution can explain differences of stage among religions but not their original and essential differences.

ent from perceptive Hinduism or Hellenism. And in all its phases Semitic religious evolution presents a peculiarity not observed in Hindu religious history. It seems, therefore, clear that as there is an element of permanence in religion in general, so there is a similar element in almost each one of the great world-religions,—an element that is peculiar to them, and that has been evolving itself through the progressive changes and the past history of these different religions. A scheme of the evolution of religion in general,—such as we have been considering up to now,—as well a study of the special elements, organic and original that differentiate one religion from another, and elements that have been persistently present in their past history, and that will persist, so far as can be seen, for ever, perhaps, in their future growth and evolution, with more or less emphasis, these are essential for the study of any religion. For it is only in the light of these that we may hope to understand both the general character and the particular and differentiating features of any religion that we may undertake to study and interpret.

Each system of religion has an essential peculiarity or differentiating feature which will ever differentiate it more or less emphatically from the others. This peculiar feature can not be overlooked in studying it.

Heredity, environment, and epoch,—these, says M. Taine, * have always played a very import-

* History of English Literature Vol II.

ant part in the development of the literatures of different nations of the world. These same elements have played an equally important part in the development of man's religion also; and they have left their mark upon the religious doctrines, dogmas, sacraments, rituals, mysteries, and the religio-ethical codes of the different races of mankind. There are very fundamental differences, for instance, between the religion of the Hindu and that of the Hebrew, as there are also between ancient Hellenism and ancient Hinduism.

Heredity, Environment and Epoch as important elements in the evolution of religion explaining both the element of permanence and that of change in them.

In the former case, as we shall presently see, these differences are due to what may almost be called organic cause,—to organic and original elements in the thought and social life of the two peoples,—they are due to what may very well be called differences in heredity, what we prefer, however, to describe as differences in race-consciousness or race-characteristics. In the other case, as between Hellenism and Hinduism, these differences are due more to environment and epoch than to any original and organic difference in the mental or social life of these two peoples. This element of what M. Taine calls heredity, but what is better understood, perhaps, by the term race-consciousness, in the case

(vii) Fundamental and permanent differences due to heredity and original differences in race-consciousness.

of the collective life of nations, constitutes the element of permanence in the evolution of the different religions, as well as that which differentiates them, permanently, from other religions, while the elements of change are contributed to the evolution of these religions by alterations in their nature-environment, through either natural or physiographical changes, or their migration to different and distant parts of the earth, having different nature-surroundings or in their social-life brought about either through the natural expansion of it, or through contact and intercourse, whether commercial or political or both, or even religious also, with other groups of men having a different type of social-structure or civic or economic organisation or cultivating different type of piety. What is this Race-consciousness? It is, what may well be called, the individuality of the different races of mankind. As there are evident but inexplicable peculiarities in different men, that differentiate them from other men, peculiarities both physical and mental, which constitute, really, their iudividuality, so there are also evident and inexplicable peculiarities even in the different races of mankind that may be said to constitute their essen-

(viii) The element of change contributed by alterations in physical and social surroundings or contact with other places and societies through religious, commercial or political intercourse.

(ix) Race-consciousness is the individuality of the race, an inexplicable original peculiarity that is pre-historic,

tial raciality or nationality or what we have called their race-consciousness or racial characteristics. That there are such racial peculiarities cannot be denied. When and how the human race came to be so fundamentally divided and differentiated, is a question which it would be futile, if not foolish to raise, because it is absolutely impossible to answer it. Whether the different races originated with one human pair or there were different such pairs, is what none can say, all that we see, are these differences in social character, differences that seem to be original and organic, and that are absolutely prehistoric. And viewing these differences modern Anthropology starts with not one but quite a number of original human stocks out of which the present humanity has grown. This is the furthest point that induction leads us to in this matter; to go beyond this would be vain and unverified and unverifiable speculation, in which science, at least, sternly refuses to indulge.

(x) Modern Anthropology finds it impossible to trace all physical and mental differences from a common stock and therefore begins with a number of stocks.

But whether the original stock was one or many, that there are fundamental differences between the different races of men, must be universally admitted. These differences are partly physical, differences in physiolo-

(a) Unaccountable differences of physiological structure and their ethical and ethnological results.

gical and anatomical structure, which modern psychometry has been investigating with such marvellous accuracy, and such remarkable results, both ethically and ethnologically. There are differences in the structure of the cranium and the face, in the pigment of the skin or the character of the hair. These differences are plainly visible as between an Aryan, a Mongolian, and a Negro. No one knows, or can even surmise, the origin of these structural physiological differences. They are there.—this is all that can be said. They are pre-historic, this is all that is known of them. And here all speculation is stopped.

(b) Similar differences in thought-structure i. e the cast and constitution of the type of social organisation and economy.

But these differences of physical structure are not, however, the only ones that differentiate the different races of mankind. There are equally fundamental differences among them, in regard to what may be called their thought-structure, that is the cast and constitution, so to say, of their mind and the social structure, or the orginal type and character of their social organisation and economy.

Anthropology an nfant Science.

Anthropology is still an infant science, and we do not as yet know what the possible implication of the differences in the physiological structures of the different races of men actually are, though some people do seem to think that they are an index of racial superiority and inferiority. Criminal anthropology has, no doubt, proved to a very large extent, the close and almost organic connection, that exists between the structure of the cranium and the mental and moral qualitles of men and women, in certain typical cases; and whatever truth there may possibly exist in the theory of cerebral localisation and phrenology, that the structure of our skulls, as an indication of brain capacity, has a vital influence upon our mental and moral capabilities can hardly be denied. But though idiots and what are called instinctive criminals, are marked out almost in every civilized race, by the peculiarities of their physiological structure, and especially by the formation of their cranium, the question what mental or moral significance can be attributed to the differences in the angle of the nose, the character of the facial and labial formations, the colour of the skin, or the peculiarities of the hair,—such as are observed between the Aryan, the Mongolian, or the Negro, has not yet been answered. It seems doubtful whether it will ever be answered at all.

(i) Some consider physiological structure as index of racial superiorty and inferiority.

The theory though not fully established has no doubt elements of truth in it which are being discovered by psychophysics.

But though we cannot as yet say what the

(ii) The indication of the differences of thought-structure and social life more apparent.

differences in the physiological structures of the different races of men indicate, we can say, to a very large extent, what the structures of the thought or of their social life mean.

(iii) Physiological differences visible to the eye but differences in thought structure observable in language.

The physiological structure of a man is visible to the eye. We see these structural differences as between an idiot or an instinctive criminal on the one side, and a thoughtfull, virtuous, self-controlled and respect-compelling man on the other- We see these differences also as between a typical Aryan and a typical Mongal or a typical Negro. But how do we, and where, observe their thought-structures—the original cast and character of their mental capacities?

A vigourous style indicates a vigourous mind in the individual as well as in the race.

In their language. Is it not? A man's style, if it be really his own, and not a mere imitation of some body else's —is a sure index to the character of his thought. Loose style, whether in conversation or in writing, is an almost unerring proof of loose ways of thinking. A vigorous style, similarly, indicates a vigorous mind, strong and broad mental grasp. Even in individual men and women their language is often an index to their thought-power and thought-life. So it is, very markedly, with races; the structure of their language or their dialect, betrays their manner of expressing their thought, and indicates the character of that thought. And it is in the grammar of these languages and dialects that we must look for the peculiar structure of the thought, of these different races. As Anthropology discovers the peculiarities in the physical and physiological structures of different races of men, so Philology reveals their real thought-structures. Here Comparative Philology must be our guide, for Comparative Philology reveals the structural differences of different languaes, as Comparative physiology and Comparative Anatomy reveal differences in physical structures of different animals, indicative of fundamental differences in thelr physical life and functions.

(iv) Comparative philology determines the differences of thought structure as comparative Physiology and Anatomy determine the differences in physical structures and functions.

Without entering into a discussion of the abstruse question whether thought is or is not possible without language, language, it may be safely asserted, never exists without thought. Its essence is the expression of thought, and therefore the structure of different languages must necessarily indicate the character of the thought of those who have been using them. For, these linguistic structures are not arbitrary formations, uncontrolled by any law or principle. The law of natural selection operates as much in the development of language, which may be said to be the organ of thought, as in that of the physiological or anatomical structures and organs of animals. And the essential character of the thought that seeks to express itself through a language constitutes the Regulative Idea in what may be called as Philological evolution. The structure of their language indicates therefore the character of the mental life of a people, even as that of its body indicates the character of the physical or physiological life and functions of an animal. In other words, the grammatical structure of a language speaks always of the peculiarity of the mind which it has always sought to give expression to.

The essential character of the thought of a people therefore expresses itself though the structure of its language.

---

§ 4 Language an index to the mental life.

"All thought consists, whether explicitly or implicitly, of three essential parts,—a subject, an object, and a predicate. This is, however, not merely an analysis of thought, but of language as well. For, in every completed sentence there are these three parts. And the structural differences of different language is mainly due to the different degree of emphasis that is laid in them, on one or other of these three elements of a completed thought or on one or other of these three parts of what

Analysis of thought and language.

(i) Essential parts—subject, object and predicate.

we understand and know by a completed sentence.

(ii) Structural differences of languages chiefly due to different degrees of emphasis on one or other of them.

The character of the mind or thought of a race is indicated, that is, by the position that is assigned by the genius and structure of their language, to these different elements of thought. In different languages, for instance, the common fact of a man striking another is expressed differently. In some the construction of the sentences would be—A struck B; where there is a very clear indication of (1) the agent, (2) the act, and (3) the object. It shows a clear perception of the different characters of these three elements of thought. The emphasis is here on all three elements of the sentence. There are other languages which do not allow a similar construction, and in expressing this common fact of a man's striking another man, it would simply say—B struck. And it shows that in the thought of this people the object dominates the subject. There are other languages where this emphasis would neither be on the subject, nor on the object, but on the predicate. Among some primitive peoples, for instance, we find that they have a different word for drinkiag different kinds of soup, one for drinking meat-soup, another for drinking fish-soup, a third for drinkiug vegetable soup and so on; * and it shows that the

(iii) The same expresses the differentia of the character of thought of a race.

The idea illustrated.

* See Max Muller, Science of Language.

emphasis, in the thought or mental life of this people, is neither on the subject or agent nor on the action or predicate, but on objects only, and, consequently, the same act of drinking, by the same individual, is viewed very differently by them according to the things that constitute these drinks. And these differences in the emphasis laid by the languages used by different races of men, on one or other of the different parts of a sentence, on one or other, that is, of the different elements of every completed thought, indicate the different ways in which these races have, from prehistoric times, viewed themselves and their relations with the objects and activities about them. In other words, the grammatical structures of different languages reveal the original world-idea, so to say, of the peoples to whom these languages originally belong.

The grammatical structures of languages thus express the World-idea of peoples.

Take, for instance, any of the languages belonging to what is called the Indo-Aryan group, Sanskrit, or Latin, or Greek, or any of the languages directly or indirectly derived from these, and certain peculiarities are observed in their structure which are not found in any other family of languages. The construction, "*I am*," "*Aham asmi*," meaning simple existence or being, absolutely without any reference to any action or object, is impossible in any other known group of languages.

Illustrated from the Indo-Aryan group.

In these other languages this idea of being or existence is expressed by some such sentence as—"I stand" or "I sit" &c. * In the same way it is only in languages belonging to the Indo-Aryan family that we find what is known as an appositional case, which allows such constructions as, "This is A," or "He is B," or "This man is great;" in which the idea of identity of being is expressed by a mere copula. In the Chinese language this construction is unknown, like the construction "*I am*" or "*Aham asmi.*" "Jin Ter" in the Chinese † means, thus, both what is expressed by the English "Great man" as well as by "the man is great." And all these indicate the different ways in which different peoples have, from pre-historic times, approached and sought to solve the great world-problems. These different thought-structures are indices to their different "world-ideas."

(IV) The story the pre-historic thought of a people read in the construction of language.

In the structure of a people's language, as revealed by their grammar, we thus discover the original bent and emphasis of their thought. It is here, in the construction of their language, that we are able to read the story of their pre-historic thought, even just, as in the construction of the earth's surface, in the geological structure of the different continents,

* See Max Muller's Science of Language.

† Ibid.

(V) The original bent of thought of a race thus discovered is an element of its race-consciousness.

we are able to study the course of their pre-historic growth and evolution. It is in the original structure of their language that we see how, originally before the birth of history, the earliest ancestors of the different races of mankind, standing, perhaps, "alone to the alone"—face to face with the over-whelming mysteries of the play of life and force about them, sought to understand their meaning and purpose; and thus developed or discovered the original bent or emphasis of their thought. And this original bent or emphasis of the thought of the different races of man constitutes one element of what we have called their race-consciousness.

Thus, for insfance, in the structure of the various languages belonging to the Indo-European group, we at once recognise the speciality of Aryan thought. Among this people, we find, that the spiritual and the universal has always dominated the consciousness of the material and the particular, that the emphasis of their thought has, from pre-historic times, been more on the noumenal than on the phenomenal. The consciousness of absolute being, the recognition of the self as existence, by itself, that have been the result of long generations of speculative effort among other races, seem to have been an original instinct with the Hindu or the Greek. This is a very curious fact.

But it is as undeniable as it is inexplicable. There is no conceivable period in the lifestory of the Indo-European languages, whether Sanskrit, or Greek, or Latin, when they did not allow, for instance, the very significant construction A struck B, or when they had not in use the construction, *I am* or its equivalent meaning pure existence, or A is A, meaning identity of being. Nor is there any trace of such a construction or of anything approaching it, by which mere being is sought to be indicated in any of the non-Aryan languages that we know of. In the thought structure of some races we thus find that there is an original instinct or consciousness of the self or the subject, in that of others the not-self or the object has been the dominating element, while, in that of a few so-called aboriginal races, the emphasis is neither on the subject, nor on the object but on the predicate. And these original bents of mind or thought have imparted peculiar characteristics to the entire thought life and thought-history of these peoples, and their literature, their art, their philosophy and their religion have all borne, ever and always, despite all varieties of environments and changes of epochs, the

Equal emphasis on all the three elements, the notion of Self or pure being, the identity of being are instinctive in the Indo-European races and ever present in their languages.

The spiritual and the universal dominating every aspect of their life and thought.

marks of these original casts of their mind and thought.

§ 5 Social and Economic arrangements as elements of race-consciousness.

Peculiar Social organisations and Economic arrangements of different races as original and organic elements of their race-consciousness, constituting the elements of racial differentiation.

As different races of men, thus, have their own peculiar way of looking at the world-problem, their peculiar cast of mind and thought, what we have called their peculiar thought structure, which differentiates their mental life, and their view both of themselves and of the outside world, from those of other races;—so different races of men have also their peculiar social organisation and economy, which also are as much an original and organic element of their life as are their thought-structures, and which also, constitute, therefore, elements of racial differentiation. In their thought-structures we see the way in which these different races have, from pre-historic times, sought to approach the world-problems, and to interpret their outer experiences to themselves. In their social-structures we see, similarly, the way in which, from pre-historic times, the different races of men have been seeking to realise their relations with other members of their society or community or tribe individually,

(I) The Social structures reveal the methods of realisation of the Social relations between individuals and individuals, and individuals and society.

and with that society or community or tribe as a whole. In their thought-structure we find how the different races have, from the commencement, so to say, of their life, approached the nature aspect of their Not-Me; in their social structure we see how they have sought to approach the other, social aspect, of that same Not-Me. The constitution of some societies has, for instance, been despotic, while in others it has been constitutional, from pre-historic times. What relations the thought-structures of different races have with their social structures, or whether there is any necessary connection between the two, is more than what we can, in the present state of our knowledge of pre-historic and primitive man, say. But we do fiud that among the Aryan peoples, as their thought-structure is of a decidedly philosophical or metaphysical type, so their social structure also is universally of a constitutional type, while the Semitic races have always had quite a different, that is a despotic type of social and civic Government and organisation. The King among the Semitic peoples has always been a military chief, whose word and will have been the law to his subjects. Among the Aryans, however, whether in Europe or in India, the King has

The different social structures show how the different races have approached the social aspect of the Not-me.

(ii) The relation between thought-structure and social-structure yet undeterminable.

(iii) The metaphysical type of Aryan thought-structure corresponds to constitutionalism in social structure in contrast with the despotic type of social and civic Government and organisation of the Semitic race.

been a constitutional Governor, deriving his authority from the suffrages of his peers. The tribal chiefs among Aryans have always been, peers among their peers,—the chosen heads of other heads of families, and never an arbitrary and autocratic ruler; and their functions though hereditary had never been of an irresponsible or despotic character. And this ideal of peer-hood or equality in some shape or other, whether latent or patent, unorganised, or organised, has been a universal feature of all Aryan societies. These peculiarities of social organisation and civic ideal are what we have sought to express by the term social-structure, which constitutes an important element of race-consciousness, and gives rise, along with the peculiarities of the thought-structures of different races, to all original and organic racial differentiations, presenting a special Regulative Idea, in the historic evolution of the different branches of the great human family. *

The Semitic Chief-a military Chief but the Aryan King a peer among peers.

(iv) The thought-structure and the social-structure determine the regulative idea in the historic evolution of a race and constitute the race-consciousness.

*"There is a natural variety of men, as of oxen and horses, some brave and intelligent, some timid and dependent, some capable of superior conceptions and creations, some reduced to rudimentary

§ 6 Race-Consciousness the Permanent element in Evolution.

This race-consciousness supplies, thus, the element of permanence in the mental and spiritual evolution of the different races of men. What heredity is in biological evolution, that this race-consciousness is in national and racial evolutions. Both environment and epoch help to bring out and modify this original constitution, so to say, of the different races, but do not create it. This race-conscious-

(I) Race-consciousness the permanent element in the mental and spiritual evolution of races.

idea and inventions, some specially fitted to special works, and gifted more richly with particular instincts, as we meet with species of dogs better favoured than others—these for hunting, these for the chase, these again for house-dogs or shepherd's dogs. We have here a distinct force—so distinct, that amidst the vast deviations which the other two motive forces (*surroundings* and *epoch*) produce in him, one can recognise it still ; and a race, like the old Aryans, scattered from the Ganges, as far as the Hebredes, settled in every clime, spread over every grade of civilisation, transformed by thirty centuries of revolutions, nevertheless manifests in its tongues, religions, literatures, philosophies, the community of blood and of intellect which to this day binds its offshoots together. Different as they are, their parentage is not obliterated ; barbarism, culture, grafting, differences of sky and soil, fortunes good and bad, have laboured in vain : the great marks of the original model have remained, and we find again the two or three principal lineaments of the primitive imprint underneath secondary imprints which time has stamped above them".

M. Taine History of English Literature, Vol. II.

ness forms also the base of all religious evolutions.

(ii) Environment and Epoch help to bring out and modify it.

This, and this alone, can explain the fundamental difference botween one religion and another. It is this race-consciousness which offers a reasonable explanation as to why the Hindu or the Hellenic conception of the Deity has been, from even pre-historic times, so different from that of the Hebrew or the Arabs. This element of race-consciousness persists through every change that a people may be subjected to, as a result of foreign contact or outside influence or authority. It is not even obliterated by community of creeds and cries, as is proved by the fact that a common Christian creed and cry, developed different types of Christian philosophy and Christian piety among Eastern and Western peoples. Of essentially Hebrew or Semitic origin, how it became almost fundamentally transformed and transfigured as soon as it entered into the Greek consciousness; as Roman or Latin Christianity, again, owing to racial differences, became something almost radically different from the Christianity of the Alexandrian schools. The same thing is observed also in the history of Islam, which assumed a distinctly philosophic and idea-

(III) Race-Consciousness explains this original differences between religions.

(iv) Permanent elements of race-consciousness alone can explain the wide differences among the different forms of the credal religions among different races in spite of common creeds and cries.

listic type in Persia, very different from the original Arab type. Buddhism also, the other credal religion, assumed two widely different forms, under the same creed and cry, in its Northern and Southern schools. And all these divergences even in these credal religions are traceable only to differences in racial or national constitutions and characteristics,—to what we have called, race-consciousness.

(v) The original conceptions of the Super-natural as well as the original ideals of social life are both essential permanent elements of religion.

Indeed, such divergences are inevitable. For, religion being essentially a matter concerning man's thoughts and sentiments on the one side, and the ideal of his relations with and behaviour towards other men on the other,—it being, in other words, a thing that relates him on the one side to what may be called the Super-Natural, and that seeks, on the other, to regulate his associations with and obligations to other members of his tribe, his community, his society, or his Church, can never divest itself altogether, either of the original conceptions of the Super-Natural or of the original ideals of social life and duty, that he inherits from his race or nation. Even among men and women belonging to the same society and inheriting the same culture and civilisation, ideas of religion are almost always found to vary

(vi) The ideas of religion ever veriable with the veriation of these elements in races, nations, families and individual.

more or less widely, owing to variations of intellectual endowment or attainments and moral culture. Even in the same family, the religion of little children must, necessarily, be different from that of adult peoples, and though all may use the same terms or receive the same sacraments, or adopt the same symbols, these have, almost universally, special meaning and significance to different persons, according to their culture, their character and the general experiences of their inner and outer life. And the story of the boy who being told that God was his father, at once shuddered at the idea, and said if that was so, he must hate God, because he would be sure to come and beat his mother,—reveals a universal truth. We thus find that among primitive races, God is very rarely addressed as mother, which is due to the degraded and helpless condition of women among them. God as mother is also unknown among even more advanced peoples, who had, somehow, come to cherish a very low and beastly idea concerning the functions of generation, and consequently also of maternity. In the Old Testament, for instance, we find the Deity repeatedly addressed as the Lord, the King, the Saviour, and as in the Book of Solomon, even perhaps as Lover, but never once as mother. This is common to all Semitic records. Islam would not address God as either Father or Mother, and in the most devout and ecstatic experiences of Islam, God is addressed only as Friend, but never in the terms of the filial or the nuptial relation. And all these go to show that whatever ideas and ideals concerning religion may be presented to man, there is always, what may well be called a law of natural selection operative in his acceptance of them, and he accepts these ideas and ideals, whenever he accepts them at all, only in his own way, according to his own light,—that is in the way that will fit them in with his general notions of things and his ideas and experiences of his special social or domestic relations,—and he always puts his own meaning and interpretation upon whatever may be presented to him as even universal truths.

(vii) Religious ideas and ideals have reference inevitably to our social life and they are interpreted always in reference to the experiences of social and domestic life.

Peculiarities of race-consciousness have, thus, a very potent and powerful influence, not only in the development of all ethnic religions, but they largely modify even the meaning and message of credal religions when these are presented to and accepted by alien races,—that is by other than those out of whose original ethnic systems particular credal systems may have at first grown in the natural course of its evolution. And a truly scientific study of the religious phenomena must start, therefore, with

(viii) Racial characteristics modify not only ethnic religions but also credal religions especially when they are accepted by alien races, giving peculiar meanings to their ceremonies and symbols.

the study of these racial characteristics. For it is this study alone that can accurately fix the meaning and significance of the religious terminology, the religious symbolism, and the religious rites and ceremonials of different races. Any other course is bound to lead to gross misconceptions and outrageous misinterpretations and misunderstandings.

Take, for instance, that much discussed passage in the Old Testament, *I am that I am.* When deputing Moses to the children of Israel then living in the bondage of Pharaoh, this is the name, in which Yahveh or Jehovah said he should be indicated to his people. "I am that I am" hath sent me to you—this was how Moses was asked to go and appear before his people. * Now, what is the meaning of this new name which Yahveh assumes here? What does *I am that I am* signify? It is clear that Yahveh, the name in which God appears to Moses, was unknown to the Israelites. He says, indeed, as much. In the earlier books, the usual name for God is Elohim or El Elohim, rendered by the English translators into the Lord or the Lord Almighty. In fact, scholars are now almost unanimously agreed that in the existing Old Testament there is a clear collation of three different sets of

E. G. The name "I am that I am" in which Yahveh asked Moses to indicate Him to his people instead of using *Elo him* found in earliest records or Yahveh in which He appeared before Moses himself.

* Exodus.

ancient Hebrew records ;—one set being called *Elohistic*, *i. e.*, which invariably describes the Deity in the terms of *El* or *Elohim*, a second set being called *Yahveistic*, wherein the Deity is named Yahveh or Jehovah, and a third set which contains directions for ritual and conduct,—the laws of Israel, and called, therefore, *Priestly Code*. * The Book of genesis is entirely based upon the first and the third of these original records. It is in Exodus that we clearly come, for the first time, upon the Yahveistic records. Yahveh, whencesoever it may have been derived, is professedly a new name among the Israelites, first introduced, evidently, under Mosaic Dispensation, —new, that is as compared to the older and more familiar El or Elohim. El, indeed, is the common term for the Deity in all Semitic languages. We recognise it in Arabic Allah, as much as in the Hebrew Elohim. Yahveh, however, seems to be peculiar to Israel, introduced into Hebrew tradition along with that of the Mosaic Dispensation. We know, however, as yet absolutely nothing as to what Yahveh meant. We cannot, as yet, refer it to any actual experience, as its source, just as we can the Sanskrit Deva or the Greek Deos or Teus. For we have the secret in the Sanskrit root *div* to give light. Deva means, thus, the bright one, the shining one, and

* Driver—Old Testament Literature.

its origin, clearly, was in the phenomena of light and darkness as observed in the heavens. Similarly we can trace the genesis of the word for the Supreme Being in Hinduism, namely, Brahman. It is from the root *Brrinha* which means large. The original idea of Brahman was thus, immensity, the all-comprehensive, the all-covering, the all-pervading, thing; and thus step by step, it came to mean that which not only covers and contains, but also explains, interprets, illumines all,—the Supreme Self, the Over-Soul, Ultimate Principle in the universe. We can trace the biography, so to say, of all or almost all these concepts. But we cannot, in the present state of our knowledge, trace the biography, in the same way, of Yahveh. But whatever may have been the origin of Yahveh, it is absolutely certain that we cannot interpret this *I am that I am* in any profoundly spiritual or philosophical sense; because such an interpretation has, absolutely, no support or justification in the thought and experiences of the Hebrew people. *I am that I am* does seem, on the face of it, to refer to Pure Being, or the Absolute, in its highest and deepest philosophical cognition; but such a supreme philosophic or spiritual instinct as could account for the growth of so abstract a concept at such an early period of their evolution, was never known to be possessed by the Hebrews. Either the new name was bor-

It can not have any Spiritual interpretation; it can not mean the Absolute as that would be inconsistent with the nature of the Hebrew race-conciousness-so much external and shallow.

rowed from some other people more philosophically endowed than the ancient Israelites, or it meant something very different from what we understand by a phrase like *I am that Iam.* Conception of the Deity as pure being could only grow among people who had a profound spiritual conciousness, and who recognised their own soul-life. Such a conception could not, possibly grow among a race that for long centuries of its thought-life had, absolutely, no notion of a future state or of any existence whatever, possible for man, apart from and independent of the body and its diverse organs and functions. And it is well-known that the Hebrews had no idea of a life after death before the Babylonian captivity, and even afterwards their conception of a future-existence was always associated with the resurrection of the human body. In the older records there is, no doubt, frequent reference to what is called the Judgment Day; but this Judgment Day refers, as a critical and careful examination of these texts distinctly proves, to this, and not, as in the New Testament, to the next life. In fact, even Jesus's teachings concerning the life of the spirit was woefully misunderstood and misinterpreted by the general body of his own people, and some scholars have even attributed his crucifixion to the ill-feeling produced by the disappointment of his earlier admirers caused by this misunderstanding. For the Messianic Prophecy which Jesus sought to interpret, did not, as understood by the Hebrews, refer at all to a Kingdom of God in the spirit of men, but to a Kingdom of God, visible and manifest, among his old and chosen people in Israel,—a kingdom that, once more reviving the old theocracy, would put an immediate end to the sovereign, earthly, authority of Rome over the Hebrew nation. Jesus's preachings of the Kingdom of Heaven, evidently appealed to the patriotism of the Jews, offered them an almost immediate release from the Roman Yoke; and this was, some say, the main cause both of his early popularity among his own people, and of his subsequent downfall; and it would be impossible to deny at least the plausibility of this view. Be that as it may, however, the fact that the Israelites had never any great spiritual or metaphysical instincts can hardly be gainsaid, and how the revelation of the concept of Pure Being, such as a philosophic or spiritual interpretation of *I am that I am* would indicate, came to be made at such an early period of Judaic history and evolution, seems absolutely inexplicable and inconceivable. Judging from the general thought-structure and religious life of the Hebrew people, such an interpretation would appear to be as reasonable and legitimate, as a highly refined and sensitive chromatic or acoustic interpretation of an utterance of Hebu Keller, the gifted deaf and blind young German lady, would be. And such misinterpretations are entirely due to the study of the religious records and experiences of one people with the help of the generalisations of those of another.

In fact attempts towards a scientific study of the religious experiences of mankind have hitherto failed to so large an extent, and have so frequently led to erroneous interpretations and unwarranted generalisations, mainly owing to the ignorance or neglect of theologians and philosophical writers, of the vital relations existing between the religious ideas and sentiments of a people and their special race-consciousness or race-character. The Right Rev. Dr. Boyd Carpenter in his Bampton Lectures, * divides the great world-religions, for instance, into two broad classes—(i) Religion of Law or Legalistic Religion, and (ii) Religion of Fellowship. Under the first head he puts in Judaism, Christianity. Islam, and Buddhism, and under the second, Hinduism or Brahmanism. Apparently the division would seem to be perfectly reason-

(ix) Ignorance or neglect of the vital relations between religious ideas and sentiments of a people and its special race-consciousness or race-character often lead to erroneous interpretations and unwarranted generalisations.

E.G. Dr. Carpenter's broad classification of religion into Legalistic religions and religion of Fellowship.

* Permanent Elements of Religion. Bampton Lectures by Bishop Carpenter.

able and justifiable, but only apparently. For though there is a kind of legalism, no doubt in Buddhism, it is essentially different from that of Judaism, Christianity, or Islam ; and the difference is brought out only by an examination of the race-characteristic or race-consciousness of the Hebrew or the Arab on the one side and of the Hindu on the other. Both the Hebrew and the Arab belong to the same stock, their languages have the same origin, the same structure, the self-same alphabet even. That is, they have a common thought structure. The social structure of the two peoples is also the same, of the military and despotic type, inspite of the fact that among the Hebrews it assumed a theocratic character. And the race-consciousness of the two peoples being thus the same, it is not at all surprising that there should be an essential similarity in their religions also, however widely the forms of these might differ from one another. Judaic and Islamic legalism can thus, very fairly, be classed together. As for Christianity owing to its origion, its legalism also does bear some similarity to that of Judaism, or Islam, though on account of the profound influence that Greek thought and culture had in the development of Christian doctrine and Christian piery, Christian legalism, in some of its deeper aspects, is yet

Unity of race-consciousness among the Hebrews and the Arabs explains the essential similarity in their religions.

slightly different also from either the Judaic or the Islamic legalism. But can we, in any away, place Buddhistic legalism in the same class? There is a kind of legalism in Buddhism, no doubt, but is it of the same character as the legalism of Judaism or Islam or even of Christianity, with which it bears in other respects, some strange similarity? In one sense, Buddhistic legalism is much more rigid than Judaic, Islamic, or Christian legalism. In Buddhism, there is absolutely no getting out of the law, except through the law itself. Here, especially in the Southern School, there is no room for grace to suspend or annul the law. The Buddhistic law is absolute and inexorable. Yet this rigid and unbending legalism is fundamentally different from the Hebrew, Christian, or the Mehomedan legalism, with which Bishop Carpenter seeks to classify it. And this difference is due to the difference in their origin,—the difference in the race-consciousness of the peoples among whom these different religions took the birth. Law in Judaism is essentially the imposition of an outside will and authority. It is, really, an outside law. Indeed, for long centuries, Judaic law never sought the sanction or support even of the inner consciousness of the children of Israel. Its conceptions is that of a contract. Its obligations are

But Buddhistic Legalism is essentially different, as it involves a very different race-consciousness.

It is decidedly more rigid but not at all external or contractual as in Judaism.

what may be called covenantal or contractual. The Lord promised certain things to the children of Israel on their doing certain things to him: this is essence of the Hebrew Law. Hebrew legalism is contractual, covenantal, associated with rewards and punishments, that are essental elements of it. This is the rudimental idea equally of Christian and Mehomedan legalism also. But the character of Buddhistic legalism is very different, indeed, from this. Here there is absolutely no conception of an outside authority which imposed the law, no idea of a personal will enforcing itself upon another. The Buddhistic law is impersonal, absolute, eternal. Its progression is like that of the tree from the seed, and the seed, again, from the tree. Law, in Buddhism, is conceived as a wheel. A wheel is a circle, and a circle is the only figure that suggests infinity * —endlessness and beginninglessness. Every point in the circumference of a circle is its beginning, and that self-same point, again, is its end also. So also with the Wheel of Law, every point is its beginning, and every point its end.

Law, in Buddhism, conceived as an infinite and eternal Wheel of which both good and evil are spokes creating *Karma* and thus causing bondage.

Law is associated, here, in Buddhism to really neither rewards nor punishments. There are antecedents and consequents: there is causation. There are causes and effects. But

* Emerson. Essays, Essay on Circle.

every effect is like every other effect, a source of bondage, becomes in its turn a cause producing other effects, to become fresh causes, again. And so on the wheel moves endlessly. What Judaism or Christianity or Islam would call good or what they would call evil, are both equally spokes in this Eternal Wheel, both create *Karma* and bind man to this inexorable and endless chain. In Judaism, or Christianity or Islam fulfilment of the law is the ultimate end. In Buddhism, not fulfilment, for the fulfilment of the end is in the generation of the tree which fulfils itself again in the production of new seeds, for producing fresh trees,—but the annulment, the destruction, the absolute cessation of the law is the goal. This is salvation. This is *Nirvana*. And when we thus carefully analyse the conception of Law in Buddhism, we find how essentially different it is from Judaistic, Islamic or even Christian legalism. Taking the ordinary classification of our mind into the Reason, the Will and the Emotions, it may well be said that while Judaic or Arabic legalism belongs to the domain of the Will, that of Buddhism belongs to the realm of Reason. The one is almost external, the other is

Fulfilment of the law, the end in Judaism, Christianity or Islam.

The absolute cessation of law, the goal of Buddhism.

Judaic or Arabic legalism belongs to the Will but Buddhistic legalism belongs to Reason.
The former empirical, the latter philosophic.

positively internal. The one is distinctly empirical, the other is essentially philosophic. The two stand on altogether different planes and can never be placed in the same class. And the difference between them is due to the different character of the Hebrew or Semitic and the Hindu or Aryan race-conciousness.

The Buddhistic legalism is one with the Hindu idea of inexorable and self-caused *Karma.*

For Buddhistic legalism is not entirely Buddhistic either. It is, in some sense, common to both Hinduism and Buddhism. For though as Bishop Carpenter says truly, Hinduism is pre-eminently a religion of fellowship, it is equally also a religion of law or Karma. And the doctrine of *Karma* is common to both Hinduism and Buddhism, and Karma is absolutely inexorable in both. Karma is also self-caused in both the systems. * And is destroyed only through illumination or *Buddhatwa* † The Hindu conception of salvation or *Moksha* is in this respect the same

The conception of Nirvana has many elements in common with the Hindu idea of *Kaibalya.*

* न कर्त्तृत्वं न कर्म्माणि लोकस्य सृजति प्रभुः ।
न कर्म्मफलसंयोगं स्वभावस्तु प्रवर्त्तते ॥
नादत्ते कस्यचित् पापं नचैव सुकृतं विभुः ।
अज्ञानेनावृतं ज्ञानं तेन मुह्यन्ति जन्तवः ॥

Bhagavad-Gita V. 14, 15.

† यथैधांसि समिद्धोऽग्निर्भस्मसात् कुरुतेऽर्ज्जुन ।
ज्ञानाग्निः सर्व्वकर्म्माणि भस्मसात् कुरुते तथा ॥

Bhagavad-Gita IV, 37.

as the Buddhistic conception of *Nirvana*. The beginningless and endless chain of cause and effect must be broken up, in both the cultures, before salvation is attained. So Buddhistic legalism is not really un-Hindu, nor is Hindu fellowship absolutely foreign to Buddhist thought, for *Nirvana* is in some sense, the same really as *Laya* or *Kaibalya*, or the losing of the individual soul in the Universal soul. And in both Hinduism and Buddhism there is the dominating Aryan instinct of the Spiritual and the Universal, clearly manifest. This sense of the spiritual or the Universal transcending the material and the particular, the common element of Aryan race consciousness, has imparted its distinctive features to the Buddhistic conception of law, making it so essentially different from the Judaic, the Islamic or the Christian conception. And the confusion into whieh Bishop Carpenter fell, in taking Buddhistic legalism as belonging to the same class as Judaic, Christian or Islamic legalism, is entirely due to the wrong method of investigation generally followed by the European students of comparative religion.

In both Hinduism and Buddhism the dominating Aryan instinct of the Spiritual and the Universal manifest.

The peculiar character of Buddhistic legalism due to its origin from Aryan race-consciousness and Dr. Carpenter is wrong in classing it with the Hebrew or the Islamic legalism.

7 A true application of the psychological and Histrio-Comparative methods discovers that religion is man's attempt at adjustment to the Not-me.

The generalisation that will discover the permanent elements of the religious phenomena presented by the history of the human race, must be based upon a much wider range of religious experience than is covered by what are known as the great world-religions. It must explore every form of religion from the most crude to the most refined and subtle. Starting with primitive culture it must trace the evolution of the religious sentiment up to the highest point as yet reached within our knowledge. It must study the history of the different religions in the light of the general laws of psychological evolution. And it must apply the comparative method in conjunction with the Historic method, in its researches into the law of religious growth. And by this means it will discover that as there are permanent elements in the general religious experiences of the race, which establish the essential unity of the religious phenomena, so there are permanent elements in every religion also, that may be charac-

(i) The permanent elements of general religious experiences and regulative ideas in the history of the evolution of every religion discovered by a phychological study of all different kinds and Stages of religious experiences by the application of the histrio-comparative method.

terised as the Regulative Ideas in their respective history and evolution, and that constitute, thus, what may be called the individuality of these religions and differentiate them from the others. We have briefly considered both these elements in the foregoing pages. We have seen that the highest and broadest generalisation that can be arrived at, by an examination of the religious phenomena *in generol*, is that religion is man's attempt to adjust himself to his Not-me, with a view to realise the highest end of his existence. This definition covers, we claim, the entire field of the religious experiences of humanity. In primitive religion, call it fetishism, totemism, animism, ancestor-worship—by any name you please,—it is man's attempt to adjust himself to his Not-me, that is to his Nature or his Social environments, that we always discover its birth, growth and evolution. There have been primitive peoples, it is said, who possess absolutely no idea of a Deity, however crude or gross. Eighteenth and Early Nineteenth century Deism, miscalled Theism, tried hard to prove the universality of the religious intuitions by attributing an original idea of a Supreme Being to every man and race, for upon such a universality it sought to build up its so-called philosophy of Natural Religion, which would preserve the truth of religion while dis-

(ii) The highest and broadest generalisation that it leads to is that religion is men's attempt to adjust himself to the Not-me.

carding the authority of supernatural revelations. The attempt was not, we are afraid, uniformly successful, for every now and then travellers turned np who testified to the utter absence of any form of religion in some one or other of the primitive races whom they had met and studied. But the battle raged, on either side around what we now recognise as absolutely mistaken issues. The old student, whether orthodox or heterodox started with a wrong definition of the Deity, some intuitions regarding whom they were seeking in primitive consciousness. God-idea as we have in civilisation could never be found in naked and cannibal barbarism. For though impious philosophers have sought to turn pious opinion into ridicule by it, it is still none the less true that if God made man in his own image, man also has always made, and is still making his God, everywhere after himself; and anthropomorphism by which orthodox theology especially in Christendom, wanted to scare away people from what is called Natural Religion, conceals a great truth which neither party seemed for a long time to be aware of. Indeed, those who admit that man is made in the image of his Maker, actuaily make over the whole case to anthropomorphism. If God made man

(iii) The attempt to base natural religion on a universal intuition of God, not always successful as it confuses the God-idea in civilization with that in barbarism

after himself, where then shall man seek and find him except in his own humanity? The study of religion in our age has, however, justified all anthropomorphic conceptions of the God-head, as the only ones that man could have of the Supreme Being. For in every age, in every country, in every place of its evolution, his religion has always been built up by man according to the actual character and the pressing needs of his physical and his social life.

(iv) Modern thought accepts that man's idea of the Deity must be naturally anthropomorphic based on the actual character and the pressing needs of his physical and social life.

In fact, religion in primitive culture is a much more vital thing than we seem to be conscious of in civilisation. With us, religion in the usual acceptation of the term is often-times a mere matter of speculation more or less, or of mere habit. We can live without it, and even die without much thought of it. It is because the problems of life are not so acutely presented to us as they were to primitive man. To a large extent we seem to have adjusted our physical life to our naturc-environments more or less, and our conceptions of what is called the Reign of Law in Nature have well-nigh killed our perceptions of the Supernatural in it. The Supernatural plays an almost infinitesimally smaller part

(v) Religion in the sense of adjustment to the Not-me is much more vital with the primitive man than with the civilised who has already got considerable adjustment.

in our everyday life than it did in that of our primitive ancestors. Every physical evil was to them due to some supernatural agency. Every illness was to them the working of an unseen agent that had either to be fought and conquered or worshipped and propitiated. Every natural cataclysm, a thunderstorm, a flood, an earth-quake, a tornado, an eclipse, jungle-fires, draughts, flights of locusts, or irruptions of wild animals,—whatever, indeed, disturbed the even tenor of their troublous life, were regarded by them as due to some active malevolent, though invisible agency, very much like themselves. As in his relations and dealings with his human enemies, primitive man had sometimes to fight them, and sometimes to sue for their favour and forbearence by offering acceptable presents to them, with a view to be able to pursue his ends in life without any molestation from them; so also he did with regard to the unseen agencies in Nature. He sometimes tried magic, exorcism, incantations, to beat these evil agencies away, and sometimes he sought to win their favour and appease their wrath by prayers, praises, and offerings. And all this was part of his rude scheme of life to adjust himself to his surroundings, and overcome the conflicts in which he found himself placed. All this was his religion. Religion was, thus, a most vital concern with

Apparent in the strong sense of the Supernatural in the primitive man.

him in the most acute and literal sense of the word.

(vi) The differentiation of our modern religious life from our physical, intellectual, aesthetic, social and even ethical life.

It is not so vital a concern in our life, because we can live without what is usually called religion. We have separated our physical, our intellectual, our aesthetic, and even our ethical life from our religious life. Not so however was it with the primitive man. To him everything was religion, and religion was everything. He was feeling his way in the dark, haunted by the fears of the Unknown at every step. We too are, perhaps, doing the same; and inspite of all our conceit of knowledge and our boasted mastery over our destinies, we too are, really, as helpless and as much at the mercy of unknown forces, so far, at least, as the ultimate issues of that life are concerned. But we are not, like the primitive man, so constantly haunted by the consciousness and the fear of the unseen. We have, at least, greater assurance than he. Our life is not homogenous, undifferentiated, like his. It has been cut up, so to say, into different compartments, of which religion occupies only one; and though we may not have the fullest freedom of that compartment, we seem to feel, at least, that we have the run of the others, and are practically absolute masters there. Loss of health or of wealth rarely drives us to religion now. We seek the aid of the physician or the financier. An earthquake, even like that of Lisbon, or more recently of the West Indies, sends us not to our gods, but to the seismograph. Religion stands, practically, divorced from our nature-environments, with which it is related still only on its aesthetic and poetic side. It stands divorced also, very largely, from even our social-environments. Our social relations are controlled and shaped now by social science, of which politics, economics, and ethics form the three chief elements, and psychology the interpreting principle. Religion is, thus, simply a matter of what may be called our private, our personal, our inner life.

Limits the scope of religion proper and makes it no longer the sole concern of our private and public life but only a matter of inner personal life.

But even in this narrowed sphere, it means, still, the same thing, namely, our attempt to adjust ourselves to our own ideas and ideals, with a view to attain our highest end in life.

(vii) But yet it is our adjustment to our ideas and ideals for attaining the highest end of our life.

But this narrowed aspect of religion among us, is, after all, a mere passing phase. We are just now passing through a differentiating phase,—a most pregnant antethetical moment, in the evolution of our culture and civilisation. Primitive religion stood in a state of homogeneity. Modern religion, especially in Europe, and generally all over the civilised world, is passing through a state of differentiation. This is, however, in its very nature, a passing state. Integration follows quick in its steps. Modern European thought even is rapidly moving towards a higher synthesis. The seers and philosophers of the last century and this, Kant and Hegel, Carlyle and Emerson, Goethe and Schalling, Tennyson and Browning, Ibsen and Tolstoi, Diderat and Whitman—are the pioneers of this new synthesis. It has commenced visibly to affect even the Churches. Both Catholicism and Protestantism are passing clearly through the throes of a new birth; and a New Orthodoxy is rising on both sides of the Atlantic, strong after a newer and loftier view of religion that will put an end to the present conflicts, between reason and revelation, science and scripture, independence and authority, and the natural and the super-natural. And it all shows that religion, even in this comparatively very high stage, means the attempt of man to adjust himself to his environments, the difference between this and primitive religion consisting only in the nature of these environments. In the earliest stage these were wholly external; at present they are mostly internal, consisting in the presentations to his own Reason of the external relation of his life, on

(viii) But the differentiation is to be necessarily followed by an integration—a higher synthesis already hinted at by the Seers and Philosophers of the last century.

(ix) Our thought and life are moving towards a new adjustment of the different aspects and relations of our life to one another and to our modern surroundings.

the one side, and the inter-relations between his intellectual, his æsthetic and emotional, and his moral and spiritual experiences and needs on the other. And in this state of conflict, even these inner and subjective phenomena, necessarily, present themselves as the Not-me.

(x) This attempt at adjustment to the Not-me, the broadest characterisation of religion in terms of universal experience presenting a common factor in all religions and in the different aspects of a religion.

This, then,—this attempt of man to adjust himself to his Not-me with a view to reach his highest end in life,—is the broadest and most universal and as it seems to us, the most rational and scientific, generalisation of the religious phenomena. It expresses the fact of religion in the terms of universal experience. It seems to present the one common factor not only in all religions, but in every phase of its evolution, in every religion as well.

In taking up the study of any particular religion, in a truly scientific spirit, and in seeking to trace its history and evolution with a view to get at the actual truth of the experiences it reveals, we must start with this generalisation of the religious phenomena. We must view it as the attempt of man to adjust himself to his Not-Me, to realise his highest end in life. And this means that our study must divide itself into two parts, namely, first, the study of the man himself, with a view to discover the particular prism through which,

(xi) This idea should guide our study of any religion which necessarily involves the study of the special race-consciousness supplying the regulative idea and the study of the physical and the social surroundings supplying the forms which the idea takes and explaining the modifications of the original intuitions by environments.

from pre-historic times, he viewed this Not-Me ; and second, the study of this Not-Me in itself, in its dual aspect of Nature aud Society,—as furnishing the materials upon which the instincts, the thoughts, the sentiments, and the energy of this man have always worked. The study of the man will reveal what we have called his special race-consciousness, the peculiarity of this thought-life, which furnishes the Regulative Idea in the evolution of his religion. The study of his Not-me, his nature-environments and social surroundings, will not only show us the *forms* that this Idea took, but will also give us a clue to the origin and history of those modifications that may have been worked into his original intuitions by his environments, at different periods of his history.

To understand Hinduism, we must, therefore, first of all study the Hindu, from the earliest period of his life, to discover the Regulative Idea in the evolution of his special history and culture,and next we must study the *forms* that this Idea has taken, and the way in which it has been accentuated or modified from time to time by,what M. Taine would call, the surroundings of his race and the epochs of his history.

(xii) Hence Hinduism is to be understood in reference to the study of the Hindu giving the regulative idea and that of his surroundings showing its forms and modifications.

THE END.

FRAGMENT.

HINDU HISTORY—

ITS BEARING ON HINDUISM.

Religion is not an isolated phenomenon in man's life, standing, so to say, apart from its other departments. In the earliest state of social evolution the state of homogeneity-religion, as we find in the records of every race, is everything, and everything is religion. As in the human fœtus, the liver performs not only its own proper and specific functions but also those of the other organs as well except the heart, so in the earliest state of social life, religion performs the functions of every department of that life. Science and art, politics and economics, commerce and trade,—everything is then a part of man's religion, and the supernatural, the specific element of the religious consciousness, plays a very prominent part in all these departments of the life of primitive man. Subsequently, in the gradual differentiation of the different departments of the social life, the religion or the sacred separates itself from the secular and the profane. This differ-

In the earliest state of social evolution religion prominent in every department of life and mixed up with all.

entiation has been well-nigh completed in Europe and America. But even in this state of differentiation religion, specifically so-called, can not be altogether abstracted from the other departments of human activities. Religion when standing in this ante-thetical state, concerns itself with God and man's relations with and duties to his Maker, primarily, and, in a secondary way, somewhat mediately, with his relations with and duties to other members of his society, and his race. But man's conceptions of his Maker are always coloured by, if they are not even directly derived from, his experiances of and relations with his physical and social surroundings. His physical life, the character of his Nature-environments, his social relations, the constitution of his society and his State, the general course of his historic evolution, the influences that are brought to bear upon the general development of his intellectual and ethical faculties, —all these have a vital relation to the evolution of his religion, specifically so-called. The religious experiences of any race or nation must, therefore, be studied, in the light of the general evolution of its history and culture. The general course of the historic evolution of the Hindu people, must, therefore, be a preliminary study to any truly scientific investigation

Differentiation brought about only gradually.

But religion of a race is always coloured by its physical and social surroundings.

Study of Hinduism impossible without reference to Hindu history.

of their religious records and their religious life. Hindu religion must be studied in the light, that is of real Hindu history.

A right conception of Hindu history is essential to a right understanding of Hindu religion. But where are we to find a Hindu history? One of the most convenient myths of European origin, in regard to India is that previous to the Mahomedan invasion, this country had never any reliable history of its own. The Hindus not only had no history, but never possessed the historical faculty even. Accuracy of observation and faithfulness in recording actual experiences just as they are, constitute the essential elements of this faculty; and the Hindus have been absolutely deficient in these, as a race. Every suspicion of historical verity is dispelled by the exaggerations of their imagination from even their legendary poems and stories, that supply valuable materials for the primitive history of other peoples. Uulike, for instance, the Greek epics, the Illiad and the Odyssey, the Hiudu epics, the Ramayana and the Mahabharata, furnish no reliable basis for working up even the semblance of a Hindu history of these early and legendary epochs. The descriptions of men and events in these books are often-times, too grossly exaggera-

The Hindus have no real history previous to the Mahomedan invasion and they are even wanting in historical faculty ---a myth of European origin.

Their legendary poems and stories are unreliable as containing gross exaggerations.

ted to be acceptable to the historian as even a flimsy basis for any historic construction. Whatever may be the real meaning and explanation of these so-called exaggerations, we shall not stop to discuss here. We simply admit that history, as an accurate chronicle of dates and events, is absent from the existing records of the ancient Hindu people. But this may not, we contend, imply the absolute absence of the historic faculty in this branch of the great Aryan race.

But the present want of accurate ancient records of facts may be thought as due to their destruction in times of foreign invasions.

In view of the notorious vandalism of some of the foreign invaders of Hindustan, it may not be wholly improbable that whatever annals of this kind may have existed in the royal archives or the sacred temples of the country were destroyed during these alien irruptions. Indeed, it seems rather incredible that a people, who, judged by the existing remnants of their literature, attained a very high degree of culture and made marvellous progress in almost all the arts and crafts of civilised life, never kept a record of the doings of their kings or the exploits of their warriors. On the contrary, we do know this much at least, that the court-chronicler was a recognised functionary among ancient Hindus, and Hindu archæology also furnishes, here and there, strange glimpses into the

Especially, in view of the civilisation they attained and the existence of court-chroniclers as recognised functionaries.

methods by which memory of important events or personages was sought to be preserved and perpetrated in ancient India. Apart from all this, which create, at any rate, a strong presumption against the validity of the popular European view regarding the utter lack of the historic faculty in the Hindu race,---do a catalogue of the names and dates of kings and warriors, and a record of their outer deeds and achievements, constitute the real basis, and the most valuable materials of true history? The value of these chronicles is not denied: but are they sufficient, of themselves, to fully elucidate and correctly interpret the real life of any people? Chronicles of dates and events furnish the sign-posts, so to say, of historic evolution; but these give us but little clue to the regulative idea or ideas that underlie it, and form, really, its very life and soul; nor do these truly and sufficiently explain those subtle intellectual and moral forces that really contribute everywhere and always to the making of important historic epochs. Not in so-called annals and chronicles, hitherto very frequently misread as constituting true history, but in the records of the thought-life of a people, in their general literature, in the pictures of their domestic and social ideals and activities, in the descriptions of their sacraments rites, and institutions,—do we find the most

Moreover, chronicles of dates and events furnish but little clue to the regulative ideas that form the life and soul of a race.

valuable materials for their real history. What would we know of Greek history without the help of Greek poetry, Greek sculpture, Greek mythology, and Greek philosophy? What would it avail the student of the historic evolution of the English people, if he had an accurate diary of the public events of the Elizabethan or the Victorian era, but not a scrap of the Elizebathan or Victorian literature? A record of the great Rebellion would mean but little to us, as British history, if we had not the writings of the Puritan Divines, and the products of the immortal genius of Milton, to illumine and interpret that tumultuous page of the history of England. The story of the French Revolution would simply impress upon our minds the hideous excesses of it,—if we had not the works, of Voltaire and Rosseau and the general thought-record of the French Illumination, to find us the real key to that great world cataclysm, to which humanity will be eternally grateful for some of its most precious heritage in the culture and civilisation of modern Europe. The thought-life of a people is their real life. The history of their thought is their true history. Annals and chronicles are helpful in the elucidation of otherwise

The most valuable materials for real history found in the records of its thought-life—its general literature, pictures of domestic and social ideals and activities.

Annals and Chronicles elucidate thought history by verification of facts and generalisations.

inexplicable points in this thought-history. These are needed for the verification of the facts and generalisations gleaned from, and based upon, a general study of a People's thought-life. But the sciences of comparative history, and sociology, as well as the general philosophy of history, have, to a large extent, made the students of social and civic evolution, which is or ought to be the chief theme of history, independent of these dry catalogues and descriptions of outward events. The psychological group of the sciences have been revealing to us certain universal truths and principles, regarding the course of human development in general, in the light of which we may now build up a more correct history of any people than what has been constructed hitherto as such, out of the annals of their kings and the journals of their warriors. From this modern stand-point, regarding the character and function of history, as a science or philosophy, the literature of a nation,—their poetry, their painting, their sculpture, their music, their law, their philosophies, their scriptures and their general religious works,—furnish a far true and more valuable record of their growth and evolution, than what the so-called historical records have ever been able to supply.

But they are now mostly superceded by the psychological sciences of comparative history, sociology &c. giving us general principles for constructing real history as the science or philosophy of the culture of a race.

And, so far as the thought-life of the Hindu people is concerned, we think there exist ample materials for the construction of a real history of it. The Vedas the Sutras, that contain the laws and rituals of the early Hindus, the rich exegetical literature that seems to have grown around the Vedas, and traces of which are found in the works of the Niruktakars or Vedic lexicographers; the Upanishads, so rich not only in their profound metaphysical speculations, but also in anecdotes and stories that throw a lurid light upon the social and civic life of the Hindus of that great speculative period; the philosophical or metaphysical speculations that subsequently grew around these Upanishads; the Puranas, representing not only the highest, the fullest, the most universal, and spiritual phase of what may well be called Imaginative or Idealistic Hinduism, but also giving a vivid picture of the social life and civic government of medieval Hindus; classical dramas; the later philosophical speculations like those of Madhavacharya, (the auther of Sarvadarshana samgraha), and Bijnanabhikshu; of Sankara and Ramanuja; and finally, the varied Vernacular literatures that developed, in every part of India, under the Moslem rule,—

The whole of the Vedic and Vedantic literature, the Puranas, the classical dramas, the later philosophical speculations and the varied vernacular literature of the different parts of India and, last of all, the architectures furnish the richest materials for such a true history.

the latest works of Tantrikism and Vaishnavism in Bengal, of Saivaism and Vaishnavism in Southern India, the literature of the religious movements of Kavira and Ramananda in Nothern India, that of Guru Nanak and his successors in the Panjab, the Abhangs of Tukaram in the Mahratta country ;—all these, not to mention the revelations of Hindu or Hindu-cum-Dravidian architectures of Southern India, Bombay, or Orissa, furnish the richest possible materials for a true history of the Hindu race. A good portion of ancient Hindu records and a good deal of the ancient monuments of this people, have no doubt been lost duriug the first period of Mahomedan invasion and conquest.

Though a good portion of Hindu records were lost during the early Mahomedan invasion.

We have, for instance, no records of Hindu painting, though it seems clear. from occasional references to it in some of our classical books, that even the art of painting had attained a fairly high degree of perfection among the mediæval Hindus. There are similar indications of the astronomical, the physiological, the physical and the chemical investigations of this people ; and as we already have through the labours of Dr. P. C. Ray, a history of Hindu Chemistry, so before long we may also have a history of Hindu physics, Hindu Physiology, and real Hindu Astronomy treated

Modern researches discovering many side-lights to such a history.

apart from Astrology. Bu apart from these side-lights that a patient study, in a Scientific and critical spirit, of the ancient literature of the Hindus might throw on their general culture and attainments, even the books that are already accessible to us, furnish fairly ample material for building up a real history of this people from the earliest times.

The already accessible books supply ample materials.

Thus it will be seen, that even if we may not work up a connected account of the outer events of the life of the ancient or mediæval Hindus, we may well build up, with the help of existing materials, a very fairly accurate and detailed story of the evolution of their thought and culture. The Vedas, the Sutras, the Upanishads, the Puranas, the exegetical literature that grew around these Scriptures, the Sanskrit classics, and the vernacular literatures, furnish ample and varied materials, if only these could be properly collated, arranged, and interpreted, for a Hindu history, that would by no means be less accurate than what modern Hebrew scholars, like Keunen, Ewald, Robertson Smith and others, have been seeking to build up, out of the records of the Old Testament, concerning the life and thought of the ancient Hebrews.

Properly collected, arranged and interpreted, these materials are adequate to give an accurate history of the Hindus though archæological and other external researches may greatly strengthen internal evidence.

Recent researches into Assyrian, Babylonian and Egyptian archæology, and the discovery of the *cunieform* Inscriptions, have, no doubt, contributed very materially to the working out of ancient Hebrew history, verifying or correcting the theories of old historians, and clearing up many an otherwise obscure print and passage of the old records, and by this means external and objective testimony has been made largely available for lending strength and support to internal evidence and *a priori* inferences. All this is true, and the absence of similar sources of corroboration in the case of the history of ancient or Mediæval India, makes the work before the Hindu historians more difficult, demanding much greater care, circumspection, and patient research, but this difficulty does not prove the utter absence of historical materials in the records of the Hindu race. Indeed, the absence of external testimony simply proves that the Hindus had from time immemorial, been practically a self-centred people. They had but little dealings with the outside world, and barring the Greek invasion and the subsequent relations with the Scythians, the Bactrians and other remnants of the Greeko—Asiatic nations, that came and entered India from the North west, the ancient and mediæval Hindus had no foreign contact worth notice. Their method of expansion

The absence of external testimony is rather due to want of foreign contact in case of the ancient Hindus.

and colonisation,—strictly confined within the Indian Peninsula,—except the later occupation by them of Ceylon and some of the Islands of the Indian Archipelego—their ways of absorbing alien tribes and cultures, their peculiar social economy and missionary propaganda—if the term could be applied to a religion that has been almost universally described as absolutely non-missionary—all these have helped to practically obliterate all traces of foreign contact or conflict from their literature. One must dive much below the surface to discover these. For, though these traces are lost, the fact that there had been such contacts and conflicts can scarcely be denied, in view, for instance, of the undoubted Hinduisation of the whole of the Dravidian people of Southern India. The story of conversion and absorption of this people into Hinduism, if only it could be discovered, would present this great world-religion in an altogether new aspect, and throw considerable light upon some of the most interesting but obscure passages of its history. It would not only discover some of the most interesting and instructive features of Hindu culture and civilisation, but would present a unique phase of religious propagandism such as the world has

Their peculiar methods of expansion and colonisation and their ways of absorbing alien tribes and cultures, so silent and imperceptible though most effective, helped to obliterate all external traces of the few foreign contacts and conflicts they had in their life history.

perhaps, never witnessed anywhere else. But the process of Hindu expansion was a quiet, a statesmanly, a thoroughly evolutionary process, that has, naturally, left no monuments or inscriptions to glorify it. It is, therefore, useless to search for any corroboration of Hindu history in foreign annals. The neighbours of the Hindus, unlike those of the Hebrews, were almost infinitely inferior to them in civilisation and culture, and who even where they did claim a high standard of culture, as the Dravidians undoubtedly did, were quietly absorbed by their stronger neighbours, almost body and soul, so to say, all but entirely losing, therefore, all traces of their previous, independent, existence.

The modern idea of a history as an account of the systematic evolution of a particular type of race-consciousness in reference to a regulative idea.

Indeed, the modern sciences of Comparative History, Anthropology, and Sociology, which reveal the general principles of historic evolution, have, to a very large extent made the student of social and civil evolution independent, of those catalogues of dates and events which had previously usurped the name and dignity of history. The sociological and Psychological group of the sciences, have been revealing to us certain universal truths and principles regarding the general course of human progress, in the light of which, we may now build up a more correct account of their real life than what had before been furnished by the annals of their courts or the journals of their warriors. History is no longer a mere record of outer events and dates, but the story of an evolution. Its aim is to trace the origin and development of particular types of culture and civilisation, represented by particular nationalities or races, and discover, enunciate, and explain the laws and principles of social evolution. It views society not as a mere mechanical collection of men and women, thrown together by chance and living together by the needs of mere animal or physical life and that have no deeper bond of union than the occupation of a common geographical situation, or the possession of a common dialect, both, again, the result of mere chance, the work of "a fortuitous concurrence" of historical events,—but, essentially, as an organism,—having a distinct life of its own, with an organic and pre-historic end, regulating and shaping that life to its own essential needs. Mere geographical situations do not *create* national life, though they do modify and regulate more or less, the outer expressions of that life. Neither do historical contacts, whether militant or peaceful, create it, though these also have a mighty influence in shaping its course. A nation, like an animal, is subject to the laws of natural selection, and may, therefore, sometimes develop new organs and sometimes, in degeneration, even lose old organs, under pressure of external conditions, whether geographical or historical, but it never, except in the case of a total extinction, loses its original type. A nation is not a mere mechanical collection of individuals, nor is it of the nature of a voluntary association, like, for instance, a Temperance Society or a universal Democratic Federation, any more than a mechanical toy is a living creature. Every organism has an end unto itself, a regulative idea which guides and controls all its activities and the manifold processes of its evolution. Every evolution, indeed, is the evolution of an Idea. Biology has neither been able, as yet, to establish the theory of abiogenesis, or the production of life from non-life, nor has it been able to discover any differentiating element in the protoplasmic cells that gradually develop into different kinds of animal organisms. So far as our present knowledge of these cells go, there is absolutely nothing to distinguish a human cell from what is developed into a puppy or a baboon, These differentiations set in later, and the same kind of cell grows into a human baby on the one side, and into a puppy, a colt, a calf, or a monkey on the other. These differentiations could not be uncaused or arbitrary. And the causes of these differentiations must have been

It is the systematic account of the evolution of a social organism through certain circumstances and in reference to an idea or end which unfolds itself with the growth of the organism which expresses it.

present, though undiscovered, in the original cells themselves. It is this which, in evolution, we call the Regulative Idea. As in the development of a portrait, the idea formed in the mind of the painter of the features of his subject, directs every movement of his pencil or his brush, so in the evolution of an organism, the Idea of it as it is to be finally perfected, regulates every step of its growth. It is this Idea, inherent in the very life and constitution of every organism, which distinguishes these from one another, the puppy from the pony, and the baboon from the human baby. The organic conception of social evolution, the conception that societies or nations or races have, like animal organisms, definite and specific ends unto themselves,—ends that shape and control their evolution, that constitute the regulative ideas in their evolution, and that therefore, constantly, consciously or unconsciously,—and more frequently unconciously than consciously, work themselves out more or less successfully, in the life and institutions of different nationalities and races, ever since their appearances, on the arena of human history. This is the view in which History is regarded by modern thought. This new aspect of History is seen, in a somewhat crude form, in the story of the Hebrews as presented

It shows how the different regulative ideas or ends evolve different organisms out of the same original materials.

in the Old Testament. That story starts with the idea of a covenant or contract betwen Yahveh on the one side and Abraham, the father of the Hebrew people, on the other. * By this contract Yahveh takes the Isrealities unto him for a people and becomes to them "a God," in a special sense. They become his chosen people, and he their chosen God. And the whole of the history of the Hebrew race is presented in the Old Testament as the working out of this ancient covenant. This special relation between them, as a people and Yahveh, is what may be called the one permanent and persistent feature of the Old Testament records,—the one regulative idea in the evolution of Hebrew history, as painted in these. What is presented in this pious interpretation of Hebrew history, as an instance of special providence, and interpreted, therefore, in a supernatural sense, in the Old Testament records, is really regarded as

The idea of covenant between Yahveh and Abraham, the regulative idea of the Old Testament records of the Hebrews presenting in its terms the peculiar type of the Hebrew genius to be realised in its life-history.

* Genesis. XII 2, 3, 7; XIII. 14-17; XV. 1-16; XVII. 1-15; and Exod. VI. 3-8. In Exod: VI. 7-8 Yahveh says,—"I will take you to me for á people, and I will be to you a God: and we shall known that I am the Lord your God, which bringeth you out from under the burdens of the Egyptians. And I will bring you unto the land concerning the which I did swear to give to Abraham, to Issace, and Jacob and I will give it you for an heritage. See also Exod XIII. and XIX. XX.

a general principle and a quite natural pheno mena of historic evolution, by the modern Philosophy or Science of History. Stripped of its supernaturalism the Old Testament view of Hebrew history means that the Hebrews as a race had a peculiar genius, a special type of mental and social structure, a special end unto themselves, as a social organism, the fullest development and realisation of which was the universal end, the Regulative Idea of their history. What modern Philosophy of History has done is simply to rationalise and universalise this supernatural and particularistic historic perspective.

The modern philosophy of history tends to rationalise and universalise this super-natural and particularistic element in each race-consciousness.

Our modern Historical science or Philosophy of History starts, therefore, with the ultimate truth of modern Anthropology, the truth, namely, of the existence of certain original, prehistoric inexplicable yet undeniable peculiarities of mental and social structures, that constitute the special characteristic and genius of different races and nations, and that furnish the element of permanence, as well as the regulative end and idea to all historic evolutions.

Scientific or philosophical history therefore starts with the regulative idea.

The study of the historic evolution of a people must start, therefore, with an examination of their peculiar race-characteristics or race-consciousness.

as we have called it, which alone can furnish the right key to the solution of the complex problems of its inner life and outer activities, and indicate the universal trend of its past, and the possibilities of its future career. The elements of this race-consciousness as we have already seen, are two, namely thought-structure and Social-structure. The study of the history of every people must commence with an enquiry into these two vital and constituent elements of their nationality or raciality. In their thought-structure we discover their world-idea, the special view-point from which almost instinctively, they have always approached the great world-problems that faced them from time to time. It is here that we find a a key to their particular philosophy of life, from its earliest and crudest to its most refined, and even transcendental stage. It is here that we find how they have viewed themselves and the world about them, from prehistoric times. It is in this thought-structure that we see the real character of the mental and moral life of the people. Like their thought-structures, different races have had from pre-historic times, types of social organisation and social economy peculiar to them. This is what we have called their social structure. As in the thought-structure of a race we find their

Discovered in their thought-structure and social-structure even from the prehistoric days and never totally forsaking it until the race is totally extinguished.

original and peculiar world-idea, the foundation of all their subsequent philosophies and speculations,—the cast and character of their peculiar intellectual life, so in their social structure we discover their original and peculiar social ideal and economy. And it is in these,—in the thought and social structures of a people, that we stand face to face, so to say, with the Regulative Idea of their historic evolution, and discover those secret forces that have shaped and controlled the destiny of different nations and races,—forces, which though sometimes vanguished by foreign ideas and ideals, have never anywhere been completely crushed out, but that have always striven,—as long as the nation or race has not been all but totally extinct,—sometimes openly and consciously, but oftener, perhaps, insidiously and unconsciously,—to reach out, anyhow, to their original ideal and end.

The first question therefore, in the study of of real Hindu History is, what is the speciality of the race-consciousness of the Hindu people?

What is the regulative idea of Hindu Evolution?

What is the Regulative Idea, the element of permanence in their historic evolutiou? What is that which has perpetually differentiated this strange people, whom more than a millennium of foreign dominations and foreign repressions have failed to destroy,—from the other nations of the world?

What is their peculiar thought-structure, and what their special social structure?

And, as we have already pointed out, the thought-structure of a people must be studied in their linguistic structure. "We know certain forms of language," says Max Muller, "which correspond to certain forms of thought, and the relations of the subject to the objects and of the elements of perception are viewed, and consequently expressed, differently in different languages. Accustomed to Aryan modes of thought, it appears self-evident to us that a language, in order to be a language, must be able to distinguish the subject from the object,—the nominative and the accusative. But as a matter of fact, there are few languages beyond the Aryan group which have distinct forms for these two categories of thought, and where the forms are wanting there must necessarily also be the spirit absent. There, among peoples outside the Aryan group, we find that the consciousness of the subject as subject, dominating the object, has been from the very beginning very feeble, so feeble indeed that it found no place in their linguistic structure."

To be found among their thought-structure expressed in their linguistic structure.

The thought-structure of the Hindus must then be studied in the structure of their original language, Sanskrit; and Sanskrit, belongs to a large and influential family of languages, of which Greek, Latin, German, and many others, designated by the name Aryan, are members. The thought-structure of the Hindus is, therefore, generically the same as that of these other branches of the Indo-Aryan family. And the distinguishing features of this common, Aryan, world-idea is its perception of the Universal and the Absolute. The peculiar linguistic structure of the Aryans, which reveals "the consciousness of the subject as subject, dominating the object," is, in other words of a pre-eminently metaphysical cast. A hankering after the spiritual, a sense of the whole have always dominated Aryan thought, whether among the Greeks or the Romans the Saxons or the Teutons, the Slavs or the Hindus. The consciousness of the self standing perpetually not only over against, but essentially independent of the not-self, has, in some shape or other, been an original consciousness with these peoples: and though its expression has been sometimes crude and sometimes clear, and been different among different branches of the Aryan family, it has never been altogether absent from their thought-life throughout the countless centuries of their past evolution. There have been variations in the common world-idea,

Generically, the thought-structure of the Hindus is *Aryan* *i. e.* its world-idea consists in the perception of the Universal and the Absolute revealed in the linguistic structure of subject dominating the object.

among the Aryans themselves, and different branches of the Aryan family have sought to realise this common world-idea in different ways, creating wide divergences in the genius of the different nationalities of this Indo-Aryan group, but nowhere has it been ever absent, and it is owing to the persistence of this world-idea in them, that we find so strange a family resemblance in the highest thoughts and speculations of such widely different peoples as the ancient Greeks, the modern Germans, and the mediæval Hindus.

Specifically, the Greeks sought to realise the parts in the whole and hence were guided in every department of life and thought by the supreme sense of form.

This original world idea, the conception of the metaphysical whole, the common heritage of the Aryan race, found, thus, somehow, an expression among the Hindus, very different from what it has had among the other branches of this family. The sense of the spiritual and the universal took, thus, a peculiar character in Greece, very different from what it had among the Hindus, differentiating, thereby the Greek from the Hindu culture. The Greeks, for instance, viewed the Universal and the Absolute from the stand-point of the particular and the relative, the whole *through* the parts; while the Hindus took, evidently, a directly opposite stand-point, and looked on the particular and the relative from the plane, so to say, of the Universal and the Absolute. The Greeks sought to realise the parts in the whole. The characteristic element in the Greek civilisation was, thus, the consciousness of "Form." In Greece the nature elements and the social elements of the National life were all regulated by this supreme sense of "Form"—the sense, that is, of the proper relation between parts, in reference to the Whole. And the resulting achievements of the Greeks were,—special development of Logic, having reference to the essential *forms* of thinking, the categories of the understanding through which the relations in nature are apprehended and understood; the perfection of Art, having reference to the right relations between limb and limb and part and part, in the perfected and harmonious whole; the growth of a very superior kind of political structure, having reference to the just relations of individuals to individuals as organs of a self-governing State; the evolution of Ethics, which regulate the relation between individual and individual and individual and the social whole. Through this innate sense of "form," Greece was able also to enter into a close kinship with all the relations of Nature in the physical world, and thereby, through close observation, to develop the ground-principles of Science.

Hence the development of Logic and perfection of Art and also superior kinds of political and social structures among them.

But, for every good there is always a counterpoise of evil, and while the special emphasis that the original spiritual and philosophic instincts of the Greek people laid on what we would call the Concrete Universal, helped to develop all these peculiar excellences of the Greek thought and culture, it also, at the same time, to a very large extent, weakened their hold on the Transcendental. And, the result of it was that the Greek conception of the God-head, even in its highest philosophic stage of speculations, was more immanental than transcendental, the Creator was counterminous, so to say, with his creation, and consequently the higher forms of God-consciousness seen in the Hindu is absent in the Greek. In Art, similarly, Greece represents the classical stage, where there is absolute harmony between the form and the spirit of beauty it seeks to reproduce ; but after the classical there is a higher phase of æsthetic evolution, wherein the spirit transcends the forms,—the phase, namely, of the romantic, which had hardly been reached by Greecian Art. In society, again, Greece recognised simply the dependence on and subordination of the individual to the Social Whole, of which they were limbs and parts, but had no consciousness of the fact that the individual too had an end unto himself or herself,

But the Greek emphasis on the Concrete Universal, the immanental, weakens their hold on the Transcendental and hence the absence in them of the higher forms of God-consciousness, of the sense of the romantic in art, of the grasp of the transcendental aspect of the human personality.

an end which is only furthered, but not destroyed or even actually overruled by his subordination to the Social Whole ;—an end that the latter cannot safely or justly ignore or usurp. In other words the Greeks had not a strong grasp of what may be called the transcendental aspects of the human personality. Whoever did not contribute to the general well-being of society, as that well-being was apprehended and understood by them, was regarded by the Greeks as having little or no claims to existence, just as an effete or paralysed limb has no right to burden the body. That absolute sanctity of human life as human life, that majesty and inviolability of the human personality as a human personality, to which Europe owes so much of her later progress and civilisation, almost in every department of life, are the special contributions of Roman law and Christian ethics, and Greece lacked these conceptions almost entirely. * All these are the limitations of Greek culture, due to the peculiar form that its original sense of the Spiritual and the Universal, the common characteristic of the Aryan race-consciousness, took—due to the fact that Greece

* And it is noteworthy also that the conception of personality in Europe, was originally not a philosophical, metaphysical, or religious conception, strictly speaking, but a more or less political idea only, basing itself upon the conception of individual rights, as citizens of a self-governing State.

apprehended the Whole, only through the relations of life and nature, and not as existing in itself, apart from and transcending all relations.

But the Hindu genius saw the Universal in the particulars as their regulative idea.

Among the Hindus, on the other hand, the same spiritual or metaphysical consciousness, the original feature of this race-consciousness, found a different expression. The Greeks conceived the parts in the whole, the particular in the Universal. The Hindus saw the Whole in the parts, the Universal in the particulars; to see a single man was to realise the presence of Humanity, because Humanity is to the Hindus in truth and reality, in all its fullness, in every human unit, however unmanifested it may be to our uncontemplative and uninstructed vision. For, is not the whole in every part of it, as its regulative idea, its end, as well as beginning? God, says Emerson, is as perfect in the atom as in the Universe; and here the Sage of Concord reproduces the highest God-consciousness of the Hindu. Every atom contained, in his vision, the Universe. Every creature had in essence the fullness and perfection of the Creator. Where is Brahman?—asks the disciple of the teacher, in the Upanishads. The teacher directs him to bring some salt and a pot of water; and the salt is put in the water and the pot set in its place. With this the disciple is dismissed for the day.

He comes for a reply to his question the next day. The teacher wants him to bring the pot of water where he had put the salt overnight. Where is the salt? he asks. It is in this water, replies the disciple. Where, find it out,—is the next direction. The disciple says,how was he to find it out, it was in every drop of that water. It is like this—एतद्वै तत्—says the teacher. Such is Brahman, in every part and particle of the Universe.

The Upanishads find *Brahman* in every part and particle of the universe.

This is the burden of Hindu Theology almost all through. The Upanishads, representing what may be called the reflective and speculative phase of ancient Hindu thought, give clear expression to the idea, but it is present as an original and organic element in every phase and form of Hindu thought. Its lispings are heard in the Vedas—in the hymns and rituals of that period,—and it is fairly recognised in the attempts even of the primitive Hindus to read some sort of a spiritual and universal meaning even in their perceptive deities,—their sensible God-experiences. It is, indeed, strange how this people, even in that early and primitive state, rushed from the particularities about them, to an apprehension of the General, if not of the Universal.

The tendency apparent even in the primitive stage.

Thus, for instance, Agni or Fire, the first born of the gods, as he is described in the Rig-Veda, and whose identity with the physical fire is absolutely unmistakable, is soon found to have established a most significant kingship with the sun, that huge ball of fire up in the heavens, and with the lighting-god, and all these are spoken of as *forms* of the one and the same god, This consciousness of the Spiritual and the Universal is heard as a most distinct and articulate note in the Upanishads. It controls also every system of later thought and speculation, including, strange as it may seem, even those that may be called materialistic or even atheistic. And it colours every form of the religious sacraments, rituals, and mysteries of the Hindu people, including even what appears to be outwardly most gross and sensuous. Thus, for instance, the temple sculptures of Orissa and other places, that naturally give such a shock to the refined tastes and morals of Europeans and even of the English-educated Hindus themselves, were meant to serve a spiritual and ethical purpose, in Mediæval Hinduism, by creating a disgust in the mind of the devotees for sensuous and sensual enjoyments, and the contemplation of these uglinesses formed part of the spiritual discipline of monks and others, for weaning their affections away from all flesh. The Ethiopean cannot change his skin, nor the leopard his spots, nor can the Hindu get rid of this over-

The sense of the Universal and the Spiritual inseparable from the very structure of Hindu consciousness in all its stages of growth.

powering spiritual instinct,—and for the self-same reason. Because the Ethiopean's colour, the leopard's spots and the Hindu's spirituality are all special, generic, and organic characteristics of their respective kind or species.

The other branches of the Aryan race also have this common element of the Aryan race-consciousness, it is true. But as we have seen in the case of the Greeks it took a different form among them, contributing those precious elements to Greek thought and culture, that constitute at once the peculiarity and the pride of modern Western thought and civilisation which owe their origin to Greece and Rome. While the Hindus saw the Whole *in* the parts, the Greeks saw the parts *in* the whole, as we have already said, and what a wide and radical difference between the two views this simple juxtaposition makes? To see the whole *in* the parts is an essentially subjective process. It involves the negation of the particularities of the particulars, the denial of all distinctions and differentiations in the vision or idea of an undifferentiated totality. But when parts are sought for and seen as parts of the whole, they are seen as related to one another and to the whole of which they are parts. So do the particulars exist, in a series of relations, in the Universal. To approach the whole through the parts, these must be put in their right relations. Not the denial, but the fullest acceptance of the reality and validity of these relations; not their negation but proper accentuation and development of these relations,—this is the only way here. And Greek culture and Greeko-Roman civilisation, the common mother of modern western civilisation, is a most glorious example of what this phase of the spiritual consciousness naturally results in. The Hindu civilisation is an example of the opposite process. It leads,—the search of the whole *in* the parts,—to pantheism in theology, determinism in ethics, and to a fatal fatalism in the general philosophy of life. At its highest point, on the one side, it leads to absolute quietism as the goal, and monkish monasticism as the way. It is the high road to all sorts of anti-social ideals and other wordly dogmas and disciplines. It is this peculiar view of the Spiritual and the Universal that helped to weaken the sense of personality in certain directions and obstructed the due development of what is understood as the true ethical consciousness, in Europe, and of the higher forms of civic life, among this people. On the other side, if sets up the

The subjective process of seeing the whole in the parts—the vision of undifferentiated totality—as opposed to the Greeko-Roman recognition of the particulars in the Universal, has led to Hindu pantheism, determinism and fatalism and also to too much of individualism on the one hand and a weak sense of personality in certain directions on the other.

individual, as representing the whole, above all relations, makes him a law unto himself, and leads to the apotheosis of the human personality, even in its most degraded form,—as really and essentially divine, and through this to the ideal of what may be called a universal divine incarnation. *

This idea of the abstract universal alone can explain the Hindu civilisation in all its phases—its effects as well as defects.

Hindu history must be studied, therefore, in the light of this peculiarly spiritual genius of that people, and the moment we do so, we find many things that had at first eluded our analysis and our understanding, revealing their reason and meaning to us, as if by a touch of magic. This sense of the Spiritual and the Universal, which forms an organic element of the Hindu race-consciousness, viewed as what is called the Abstract Universal, explains the meaning of Hindu culture and civilisation, finds out the secret of their social economy, and their civic laws and institution, as well as of their philosophies and their religion. It is this which also easily explains and accounts for those limitations and deficiencies in their life and thought that have not infrequently led superficial

* See Geeta—IX. II

अवजानन्ति मां मूढा मानुषीन्तनूमाश्रितम् ।

परं भावमजानन्तो मम भूत महेश्वरम् ॥

students of Hindu civilisation to relegate it to a lower and comparatively primitive stage of human progress. To properly understand the meaning and significance of the historic evolution of the Hindu people, we must examine, in some detail, the results of their innate sense of the Spiritual and the Universal, in their relation with Nature, Society and God,—results that have lent a special tone and character to their physical, to their social, their intellectual, their æsthetic and their religious life.

The absolute supremacy of the spiritual over all external and objective forces the keynote of Hindu civilisation.

This sense of the Spiritual and Universal is the Regulative Idea in the historic evolution of the Hindu people. This is the prism through which the Hindu has always viewed himself, his social and his physical or nature environments. And consequently a sense of the absolute supremacy of the Spiritual over all external and objective forces, whether social or physical, has always dominated all his relations with both society and nature. Superficially viewed, social authority seems to be absolutely crushing to the individual in India. There is, apparently, but little room for the exercise of what is called personal or individual freedom in either domestic or social relations among the Hindus. Society, through its caste-codes and its religious sacraments and ceremonials absolutely dominates the life and activities of the individual to its minutest details to the extent even of his choice of food and drink even on different days, of the week or the month. The authority of Society over the individual seems, thus to be as rigid and as absolute here as it ever was among the Greeks. But this is, however, only a superficial view of the Hindu social economy. Society does control the individual here as it did in Greece, but the end was not the same in Greece as it has always been in India. In Greece the individual was considered as a limb of the body politic, and the control of the limb was regulated by considerations of the well-being of the organism, the State. In India among the Hindus, the authority of society over the individual was imposed for a different purpose. Here the well-being of the organism was not the only, at any rate it was never the supreme end in the regulation of the individual. The individual, the Self itself was that end. Society was only a school for the training of the individual,—for the development and perfection of the real life of the individual, that is, his spiritual life. Social bondage was not an end unto itself, but was only a means to a higher end, and strange to say, that

As a sample of its application—to the Greek the individual was a limb of the body politic and thus subordinate to the Society but to the Hindu, the individual, the Self itself, was the end in itself and the Society only a school for his training in and through which he has to obtain freedom from bondages by means of regular course of discipline.

end was the very freedom of the individual whom society sought so rigidly to rule. Through bondage to freedom, that was the process. Subordination to social disciplines was meant to cure the conceit of self, to bridle unruly passions, to regulate the appetites by giving *legitimate* but *restricted* opportunities for their satisfaction.

The assertion of the Spiritual and the Universal in the relations of man with his nature-surroundings.

As in his social life, so also in his relations with his nature-surroundings, this innate sense of the Spiritual, and the Universal always asserted itself. Nature is terrible, in its wild aspects, in India. Its majesty stands almost unrivalled, in the snow-capped mountains, the rushing rivers, the endless expanse of arid plains or wild vegetation,—almost all over Hindustan. But awful as his nature Nature-environments, both terrestial and celestial, have always been, the Hindu never allowed these to overawe or overwhelm him, except only as expressions or symbols of the Spiritual and the Universal. Viewed from the stand-point of the Absolute and the Spiritual, Nature appears in one of two ways. It is either

Nature viewed either as an expression of the Over-soul or as an illusion that hinders the vision of the Real.

an expression, a radiance, a sign and symbol, of the Absolute,—the outer-body, so to say, of the Over-Soul, the form which the World-Spirit or the Cosmic Soul has thought fit to assume for its own self-revelation, or self-realisation or it is an illusion, a false covering, a hideous nightmare that hinders and distorts the vision of the True and the Real. Nature stands, thus, either as a medium of communication or communion between God and man, or as a veil that shuts his God out of the sight of man. In the one case, Nature will be sought to be idealised and spiritualised, quickening and feeding the faculty of Religious Imagination, to a very high pitch, and giving birth to a most marvellous apotheosis of the cosmic forces and phenomena, both in their totality, as well as, in their varied, differentiated, and fragmentary aspects. In the other case, it will be shunned, ignored, deliberately denied and negated. But in neither case will there be any attempt or even any desire to enter into any serious conflict with Nature, with a view to its ultimate conquest and submission. And this has been the general character of the Hindu's relations with his Nature-environments, all through his past history.

But not as an independent power to come in conflict with.

In the earliest stages of his life, as indicated in the hymns of the Rig-Veda, for instance, the Hindu too had his conflicts with his Nature-surroundings. Such conflicts are universal in what is called the jungle-clearing stage, when man's first concern is how to clear the earth, both of beasts

Evidence of early conflict with nature visible in Rig-Veda but not very prominent.

and vegetation, to make it a safe habitation for himself and his kind. There are just a few Suktas in the Rig-Veda which preserve for us the memory of this period of primitive Indo-Aryan history. But the generality of the Vedic hymns belong to a later period, when the Aryan settlers in India, had practically settled down to a fairly advanced agricultural life, which implied a certain amount of progress in the arts and crafts of civilisation. The dominant note, therefore, in the Vedic hymns in regard to the view that the Vedic Hindus took of their nature-surroundings, is one of fellowship. The Vedic hymns are very largely addressed to what are called Nature-deities, representing the spirit, so to say, of natural objects and phenomena. Fire, in its dual aspect of terrestrial fire, and celestial light and heat,—is one of the most prominent of the Vedic Gods. The sun, the firmament, the clouds, sending rains and hurling down the thunderbolt, the storm winds, the morning and evening twi-light, the rivers that flowed through their settlements, fertilising their fields, carrying their primitive merchandise, and spreading their culture and their dominions,—all these and others like these, natural objects or phenomena with which the Vedic Hindu was familiar and which influenced for good or evil

The prominent relation with the forces and objects of nature is that of fellowship as is manifest in the Vedic hymns to the Nature-deities

his earthly life and happiness,—are the most prominent of the Vedic deities, and the hymns addressed to these bear ample evidence to the spirit of friendliness and fellowship, in which the Vedic poets and seers, usually viewed the Nature-forces about them.

This spirit of friendliness and fellowship with Nature-forces and natural phenomena, could not possibly grow without the very closest observation of these forces and phenomena. And an examination of the ritualism of the Vedas shows how careful had been the Vedic Hindus in their crude observation of their nature-surroundings, and more particularly of the phenomena of light and darkness, and the rains and the seasons. Astronomy—*Vedanga Jyotish*—is one of the six recognised branches of Vedic knowledge, without which the study of the Vedas could not be regarded as completed. The minutest observation, as far as it was possible with the naked eye,—of the movements of the sun, the moon, the planets and the stars, was needed for the determination of the right moment for the performance of Vedic sacraments and sacrifices. Astronomical observation became, thus, a religious necessity with the Vedic worshippers. The same need led them to the study, in their

Such a relation presupposes a more or less close study of nature as found in Astronomy, Anatomy, Physiology, Geometry &c. and developed in the Vedas as Vedanga often through the exegencies of ritualism.

primitive way, of animal anatomy and physiology, for with the growth of ritualism, there grew up a very complicated system of animal sacrifices, which demanded a very minute and careful division of the sacrificed animal body, not only for the various offerings made to the gods, but also for its division among the different orders of priests and chanters who took part in these sacrifices. Minute directions for the construction of sacrificial alters and the preparation of the sacrificial grounds led to the discovery of the elements of Geometry and Mensuration by the Vedic Hindus. And all these indicate some sort of rudimentary scientific observation and research, though conducted not exactly in the spirit of science or after strictly scientific methods, but simply prompted by religious or sacrificial and ritualistic requirements. Besides these, the very needs of ordinary human existence impelled the Hindus, as they did other human groups, to investigate the properties and character of the natural forces and objects about them. A knowledge of the seasons was necessary for agricultural purposes; that of herbs and minerals was needed for manufacturing as well as medical purposes; some knowledge of mechanics was essential to a people who built stone-structures, used cotton and woollen clothing, rode in chariots driven by

Thus originating some sort of scientific observation and research.

horses and oxen. And all these imply some knowledge of nature, some conquest of and supremacy over natural forces and phenomena. Indeed, no people could possibly attain the standard of civilisation that the Vedic Hindus seem clearly to have done, without the establishment of some sort of a mastery over nature and without wresting some of her elemental secrets from her hands.

The Scientific tendency further stimulated by the needs of everyday life and progress in civilization.

But still the spirit in which the ancient Hindu approached Nature was not in any sense, what would be called a scientific spirit in our age. The Hindu approached his nature surroundings, in the spirit of the poet and the seer,—like a painter or a philosopher. He did not botanise his plants and herbs but he simply sought to idealise and spiritualise the vegetable kingdom about him. He did not bring the sun down from the heavens and press him under the spectrum, nor did he catch up the death-dealing, thunder-discharging, and yet beneficient, because rain producing lightning from the sky, to make it run on his errands of peace or war over measureless miles of vacant space. He did not gauge the rains by inches, nor span the heavenly heights of his snowcapped mountains by the theodolite. He saw, he heard, he felt, and by his own inner

The Hindu viewed nature not as a scientist but as a poet and seer.

sensations and emotions, he sought to take his own soul-satisfying measure of the outer world. Consequently whatever records we have of the ancient Hindu's nature experience, have almost universally, which may be called a soul-reference in them, either direct or indirect. Nature was to him not a thing apart, not a thing that had a real existence outside or absolutely independent of him, but he found it, at the final analysis, when he attained the reflective phases of his evolution, to be a part, really, of the self; and by the experiences of that self, by its sensations, impressions, and emotions, he always measured Nature, and interpreted it, and to the highest ends of that self, throughout his whole history, he tried to turn it. So there is poetry even in his science; which means that he always clothed the real with the ideal, the material was always symbolised by, if not universally transfigured into, the spiritual. And thus the genius of this race asserted itself even in its experiences of and relations with their physical surroundings.

So he could not so much utilise the the forces of nature in his external life as he could read his thoughts and emotions in them.

He conceived nature as a part of the self and always clothed the real with the ideal.

This curious admixture of science and poetry, common to all primitive culture, has, however, a peculiar meaning and significance in the case of the ancient Hindu. It is not the product of wild and untrained imagination. In fact, this is found in records that must have grown side by side, almost with some of the profoundest speculations of the Hindu mind, speculations that reveal the wonderful analytical powers of this race ; and when, the Hindu intellect could hardly be called, therefore, very wild or untrained. Nor is it the product of what has been termed, with ill-concealed contempt, as "oriental imagination"—which is an euphemism, plainly, for deliberate falsehood or lying exaggerations. But it is the product, really, of the innate sense of the spiritual and the universal, of this people. What unimaginative European critics condemn as "oriental imagination," is really the result of idealisation and spiritualisation, even though it should seek to express itself in the terms of the material and the sensuous. And it would not, we contend, be very easy to determine whether the highest truth is to be found more in what people usually characterise as *real* than in what the unimaginative and the unspiritual necessarily dismiss as mere *ideal.* Usually we declare our sense-testimony only as real. For purposes of strictly scientific investigations this definition of the real is correct *tentatively*, and absolutely *needed.* But people who take the testimony of the senses, what is called scientific

This poetic element in his science is not the product of wild imagination but is really idealisation or spiritualisation.

evidence, as absolutely real and true, forget the tentative character of it, as well as ignore the narrow limits within which the sciences have necessarily to work. For are our senses the only, or the highest witness of reality? What, indeed, is sense-testimony itself, except the *impression* produced upon a sentient being by the contact of sense-objects with his senses? And these *impressions* are measured really not by the senses,—the senses only communicate impressions but do not record them—but by the mind, their universal reader. What happens, really, in so-called strictly accurate or scientific statement or record of our sense-impressions is that the mind works here within certain arbitrary limitations, and reproduces not the whole but simply a part of the impressions of sense-objects communicated to it by the senses. Generally speaking, science, by its quantitative and qualitative analysis, limits the mental records of sense-impressions to their relations in space and time, ignoring for the time being, that both extension and succession, implying relations, are apprehended, not by the senses, but by the mind alone. Thus, in what are called strictly accurate records of outer objects and events, the mind divides

The tentative character of scientific evidence to be always supplemented by the interpretations of the the sense-impressions by the understanding.

Science is concerned with a limited view of things in space and time which are really apprehended by the mind.

itself, so to say, from itself, and gives out, not the whole of its impressions, but only a part, and really, a very contemptible part of them. In fact, mere sense-impressions do not constitute knowledge at all ; nor is such knowing, if knowing it may, at all, be called, in any sense, an evidence of the truth even of external objects. Perception, emotion, and volition these are the three essential constituents of knowledge, and truth or right knowledge is established only when perception is followed by its own proper emotion or feeling, and finally, when this emotion or feeling is followed by volition or activity, and when this activity is justified by the actuality of the thing perceived, it is then only that the real truth of a thing may be said to be thoroughly established. This is the test of truth as recognised, at least by Hindu Logic. And this canon is equally supported by the highest methods even of modern science. How, then, can we abstract the feelings that particular sense impressions produce from our real knowledge of sense-objects ? What is called ordinarily accurate statements is only, thus, a partial record of our impressions of objects and events. It is an outside measurement of them. The sensorium or the *Manas* measures things from the outside, the heart measures them from the inside.

Perception constitutes true knowledge only when followed by emotion and volition and volition justified by the actuality of the thing perceived—the test of truth in Hindu Logic.

The one refers them to things conceived as standing outside the seer or the knower: the other refers them to the seer or knower himself. And why should the one measurement be declared as true and accurate, and the other as false, exaggerated, and fanciful? The one, really, is the result, of the materialisation of the mind, so to say; the other the result of the spiritualisation of matter. This is the difference between Western truth and Oriental imagination. And this fact must be borne in mind in studying Hindu records, whether they refer to scientific, historic, literary, or religious subjects.

The Oriental imagination spiritualises matter while Western Science materialises the mind in its method of studying objects.

The fact, really, is that what is contemptuously characterised as "oriental exaggeration" is only the preponderating soul-reference or subjectivity of these records, indicating the overwhelming sense of the Absolute and the Universal that possessed the Hindu mind almost from prehistoric times. In the earlier stages of their historic development, the vehicles of their thought were, naturally, not only crude, but also exceedingly limited; and the expression of their sense of the Universal and the Spiritual, by means of such crude and chaotic materials as were supplied by their natural or social environments, naturally

Thus the oriental exaggerations really refer to the preponderating soul-refernce of the Hindus even from prehistoric days though the expressions were then necessarily crude and defective.

became somewhat chaotic, crude, and exaggerated. Hegel's characterisation of the first stage of the evolution of art, as *oriental,* in the sense which he uses the term, is, therefore, hardly applicable to Hindu art, be it poetry, or painting, or sculpture or architecture.

Hindu art not *oriental* in the Hegalian sense of *form* overwhelming *spirit.*

Oriental art, according to Hegel, is that wherein the *form* overwhelms the *spirit.* But in the consciousness of the Hindu,—the form never, actually, overwhelmed the spirit, but it is rather the *spirit* that overwhelmed the *form.* Philosophy of Art characterises it, rather as the third,—according to Hegel the highest,—stage of the development of Art.

In it the spirit overwhelms the form.

In saying, however, that even in the earliest stage of Hindu art, the *spirit* overwhelmed the *form,* we do not mean to claim for it, really, a place in what is called, Romantic-art. In Romanticism the spirit overwhelms the form of art, in a way very different from that in which it is found, actually, in ancient Hindu art.

Though it can not be placed in the Romantic or even the classical stage of development.

Romanticism is preceded by classicism,—the stage of art-development, wherein there is an equipollence of form and spirit—"a balance, a harmony, a reposeful interpenetration of form and matter." In romanticism, we have a distinct "*transcendence* of the matter by the form" of the symbol by the soul. In the earliest Hindu art, we do not find this *transcendence*, which is characteristic of real romanticism, but simply an overwhelming of the form by the spirit :—an attempt to overcome the symbol by the soul. In fact, since the entrance of Japanese culture and Japanese ideals into the common room of European culture and ideals, even European art-students are being compelled, gradually to re-examine their old estimates and canons of art-criticism ; and the dominant or impressionist school of Japanese art, has already claimed a distinct place and position for itself. There is, no doubt, a very wide difference between modern Japanese and ancient Hindu art, and the two cannot by any means be classed together. But the spiritual note, the sense of the whole, almost independent of that of the relations of the parts to one another, through which it exists and reveals and actually realises itself,—is common to both. For impressionism has necessarily a soul-reference always. It realises or seeks to realise a form of beauty, not, really, as it stands in itself, in its varied relations to its own parts and its own environments,—but as the *whole*, including the relations and environments, *impresses* the mind or the soul with itself. The ancient Hindu records belong

In it the soul attempts to overcome the symbols though the distinct transcendene of the spirit over matter is not established.

In conmmon with the modern Japanese art finding its own place in Europe, the ancient Hindu art has a sense of the whole independent of the parts.

to this class. They are records not of objects or events in themselves, but of the *impressions they produced upon the mind of the recorder*. And our mental inpressions can merely be indicated but can never be actually photographed. Much less are our spiritual impressions, that are almost infinitely more complex and subtle than our ordinary mental experiences.—capable of even an approximately exact reproduction whether by words, by colours, or by hewing and carving. They can never be reproduced with any pretension to exactitude, especially, in the earlier periods of human evolutions, when the vehicles of human thought are, necessarily crude, tentative, and limited, owing to the crude and chaotic and limited character of man's experience in that primitive state. Hindu records must, therefore, be studied and interpreted not as representing the nature or social surroundings of the Hindu, as they existed, actually, in themselves, but as seeking to indicate how they *affected his inner*, his *mental, his emotional, his spiritual life*. Viewed in this light, it will be seen that despite the apparent crudities and what appear as wild and hysteric exaggerations to the modern mind,—

They are records of impressions that objects produce on the mind of the recorders. And mental and spiritual impressions can never be reproduced with exactness, especially when expressions are crude.

The Hindu records present, therefore, not the actual physical and social surroundings but their effects on the mental and spiritual life—the experiences they record are subjective though real as such.

of the ancient Hindu books, the experiences they record are subjectively real, and as such, absolutely true.

The prominence of soul-reference in Hindu thought makes the realistic descriptions of the elementals in the Rig-veda spiritual instead of material.

On account of this peculiarly spiritual prism through which the Hindu viewed everything, nature never presented itself to him as *merely* natural, nor man, either, as *merely* human. Natural objects and phenomena had always to him a soul-reference. Fire, water, ether, sky, the sun, the moon, the stars, the twilight, the clouds, the winds, the rivers,—all his nature environments, whether terrestrial or celestial, were always soul-ful, so to say, in his eye. We have some of the finest realistic descriptions of these elementals in the Rig-veda, to be fonnd, perhaps, anywhere, in any human literature, ancient or modern. But this *realism* is not *materialism* in any sense of the term. The pictures have always a halo of genuine spirituality about them, The poetry of the Rig-veda, indeed, defies Hegel's classification. It is not, really, oriental,

The poetry of the Rig-veda is neither oriental or classical or Romantic in the Hegalian sense but forms a distinct class by itself.

in the sense that the form overwhelms the spirit, the expression the ideal, the symbol the soul. It is not, in any sense, classical or Paganistic either, as having a clear conception and firm control of the relations of things, out of which grows that equipollence between form and spirit, which is the characteristic of Classicism. Nor can it be called, in any sense, romantic, either; for there is really no "*transcendence*" of the form by the spirit here. The poetry of the Rig-Veda stands, thus, by itself, as a distinct class or type, which reproduces nature through the lens of the mind, the spirit, the soul,—neither overwhelmed by its chaotic mass (which would make it oriental in the sense of Hegel); nor standing fairly balanced with it (which would make it classical); nor even exactly transcending it (which would make it romantic);—but simply interpreting it, even as it exactly stands outside, as a spiritual factor, however crude may be the conception of this "spiritual" itself.*

In which the spirit interprets nature as a spiritual factor without over-whelming or being overwhelmed by or standing fairly balanced with it.

This quasi spirituality of the Rig-veda developed into what may be called a pure, though perhaps a preponderatingly abstract, spirituality, in the Upanishads. In the Vedas Nature is, so to say, simply vitalised, on being transmuted as mental experiences, in the consciousness of the ancient Hindu. It stands here simply humanised. The view is not exactly animistic, which would raise a suspicion of the identification of life with the body,—but anthropomorphic. There is, indeed, no

* See descriptions of Agni, Varuna, Indra, Aswinikumaran, Saraswati, Rudra, Maruts &c.

suspicion of the identification, in consciousness, of the body with the life principle, of form with spirit,—in the most crude or most primitive of these records. The sense of the spiritual and the universal,—the sense, that is, of the Absolute, being an original, an organic, and pre-historic endowment of the Hindu race-consciousness, such identification of the body with the soul could never vitiate Hindu thought, even in its earliest stage. It is, therefore, that we find Tylor's animistic theory of the origin of religion, inapplicable to, and unsupported by the records of the Aryan, and especially of the Hindu people. The Vedic view of nature, we therefore prefer to characterise as humanistic or anthropomorphic. In the Upanishads it is distinctly spiritualistic or idealistic, and monistic. Nature has no existence here apart from Brahman or the Absolute. It is his covering, his manifestation, created out of himself by him, existing in him, and in death or decay, going back to and losing itself in him. Brahman is both the efficient and the material Cause of the Universe. The sun, the moon, the stars, the immensities above, and the myriads of forms and appearances below,—are all sparks of him, the

The Vedic conception of nature is thus human or anthropomorphic—interpreting nature by mind but not identifying the one with the other.

This anthropomorphism of the Vedas is developed into Idealism and Monism in the Upanisads which take Brahman both as the efficient and the material Cause of the Universe.

Eternal, the Absolute, the Infinite Being. These are reflections of his thought, endless ripples rising on the surface of his infinite energy, creations of his absolute will. He throws them out, at his pleasure, and draws them in again at his will.

The abstract Universalism of some of the later Upanisads developed the *mâyic* conception of the Universe and thus brought about a separation between the natural and the spiritual and this ultimately led to a stagnation of scientific thouht chiefly through man's weakness and inability to cope with the forces of nature.

But while there is a very distinct note of divine immanence in the Upanishads, the growth, really, of the earlier nature spiritualism, so to say, of the Vedic thought, it became gradually lost in what may be called the Abstract Universalism or the subjective idealism of the later Upanishadic speculations. The dominant note here is not of an idealisation,—what, in fact, may even be termed a distinct apotheosis of the cosmic forces and phenomena, united in and conceived as the Virata-Purusha or the Viswarupa,—of Nature, but, practically, that of the denial of all truth and reality to it. With the growth of this Mâyic conception of the phenomenal world,—wherein Mâyâ is conceived not, as in the earlier as well as in some of the later speculations, as the creative energy of the Divine, differentiated from himself in the process of his self-revelation or self-realisation, and, therefore, as a *real* and *substantive* moment of the Divine Being,—but as mere illusion,—there grew up a distinct divorce and separation between the natural and the spiritual life. And in consequence of it, after a certain stage, when nature was too strong to be ignored and man too week to meet even the essential requirements of his physical life, and of the state of civilization that he had already attained,—all progress of the natural sciences came, practically, to a stand-still.